The Guide to
WALLACE NUTTING FURNITURE

by
Michael Ivankovich

Published by:
DIAMOND PRESS
P.O. Box 2458
Doylestown, PA 18901

The Guide To
Wallace Nutting Furniture

Copyright @ 1990, Diamond Press

All rights reserved. No part of this work may be reproduced or used in any form or by any means - graphic, electronic, or mechanical, including photocopying or information storage and retrieval systems - without written permission from the copyright holder.

Library of Congress Catalog Card Number : 90-83325
ISBN: 0-9615843-7-8

**Other Wallace Nutting Reference Material
Available From Diamond Press**

Wallace Nutting General Catalog, Supreme Edition...the complete 1930 Catalog of Wallace Nutting Reproduction Furniture... by Wallace Nutting ($12.95)

The Price Guide to Wallace Nutting Pictures, 3rd Ed. by Michael Ivankovich ($12.95)

The Alphabetical and Numerical Index to Wallace Nutting Pictures, by Michael Ivankovich ($14.95)

The Wallace Nutting Expansible Catalog by Wallace Nutting, Introduction by Michael Ivankovich ($14.95)

Wallace Nutting by Louis MacKeil ($6.95)

Please add $1.25 postage and handling for each book ordered
Mail to: **Diamond Press, Box 2458, Doylestown, PA 18901**
For **Rush VISA/Mastercard** Orders, call (215) 345-6094

Michael Ivankovich also conducts periodic Wallace Nutting specialty auctions featuring Wallace Nutting Pictures...Books... and Furniture. If you would like to contact him regarding upcoming Wallace Nutting Auctions, about buying or selling any Wallace Nutting material, or simply being put on his mailing list for any future Wallace Nutting updates, you can write to him c/o: **Diamond Press, Box 2458, Doylestown, PA 18901**.

Contents

Introduction..i

Chapter 1 - Wallace Nutting...The Photographer.....................1

Chapter 2 - Wallace Nutting...The Author.........................7

Chapter 3 - Wallace Nutting and Antiques........................17

Chapter 4 - Wallace Nutting Windsor Chairs......................29

Chapter 5 - Wallace Nutting Ironwork............................55

Chapter 6 - The Transition Years - 1922-23......................65

Chapter 7 - Other Wallace Nutting Furniture.....................73

Chapter 8 - The Decline of the Wallace Nutting Furniture Company..89

Chapter 9 - Identifying Wallace Nutting Furniture................99

Chapter 10 - Recollections of Wallace Nutting...................115

Chapter 11 - Wallace Nutting Advertising........................127

Chapter 12 - List of Recent Sale Prices.........................135

Chapter 13 - Conclusion...143

Wallace Nutting (1861-1941)

Introduction

By 1917 Wallace Nutting's picture business had become more successful than he had ever dreamed. His hand-colored platinotype pictures caught the attention of an early 20th century American middle class, with literally millions of his Interior and Exterior scenes selling throughout the country.

With many day-to-day operations in his profitable picture business turned over to several key employees, Wallace Nutting turned his attention to his true love...early American antiques.

Starting with very little practical experience, Nutting began actively collecting antiques shortly after moving his picture business to Framingham, Massachusetts in 1912.

Like many true collectors, Wallace Nutting jumped into his newest avocation with a passion. First buying just one antique, and then a few more, his passion grew to where he once purchased the contents of an entire Antique Shop, just to obtain a few special pieces.

But Nutting wasn't the only person collecting antiques back then. Even as early as 1917, with the Colonial Revival Movement well under way, the finest examples were frequently unobtainable... anywhere.

Nutting was quick to recognize that if he was having difficulty obtaining early Pilgrim Century furniture, so too were other collectors. Many could not afford the finest forms and, quite often, those who could afford them...could not find them.

Beginning first with Windsor chairs, Nutting went on to gather some of the best early American furniture ever produced. He would photograph each piece and document what he saw, analyzing and measuring every leg, stretcher, spindle, and seat. He would then reproduce what he perceived to be the *perfect* piece of furniture... piece-by piece ...turn-for-turn..as close to the original as possible, using nearly the same methods employed by 18th century furniture makers.

This book is about **Wallace Nutting Bench-Made Reproduction Furniture.** It's an area of collecting that is just beginning to attract a great deal of national attention. Some people have been collecting Nutting furniture for years. Early furniture scholars such as Luke Vincent Lockwood and Francis P. Garvan recognized the high quality of Nutting's furniture even back in the 1930's. According to Ernest John Donnelly, Nutting's bookkeeper, Mr. Garvan, whose collection is housed in the Yale University Art Gallery, bought one of each Nutting reproduction.

Other individuals bought Wallace Nutting furniture not so much because they understood its technical merit, but simply because they liked the look...and it was affordable to them.

In recent years Wallace Nutting furniture has been largely ignored, primarily because most people haven't really understood its significance. I've been amazed at the large number of knowledgeable Nutting picture collectors who simply weren't aware that he also produced furniture. There hasn't been any primary source to turn to for an explanation of **what** type of furniture was produced, **how** it was made, **why** it was reproduced, and **what** it was worth...**until now**. This book is intended to explain what makes Wallace Nutting furniture so unique and collectible.

You'll notice that the title to this book is **The Guide to Wallace Nutting Furniture.** It is **NOT** "The Price Guide to Wallace

Nutting Furniture". There is simply not enough documentable pricing information to call this book a "Price Guide". Yet, although this book is not intended to serve as a Price Guide, it may end up being used as one until the Nutting furniture market becomes better defined. I expect that this book will eventually evolve into a "Price Guide" in future editions.

It should be made quite clear that every price reported in this book is either a price that someone has already paid for a piece of Wallace Nutting furniture...either at auction, at an antique show, or through private sale...or represents an asking price, set by a reputable dealer, where we were unable to determine the final sale price.

I am not attempting to set any pricing ranges or levels, nor am I trying to lead anyone to any pricing conclusions. I am simply reporting the current state of the Wallace Nutting furniture market as it exists today in order to help collectors gauge what a particular piece may or may not be worth to them.

But regardless of price, I think you will agree after reading this book that Wallace Nutting did indeed produce some of the finest furniture made in the twentieth century.

A typical Wallace Nutting outdoor, or "Exterior" scene, with apple blossoms, and a peaceful country stream.

Chapter 1

Wallace Nutting...The Photographer

As he was preparing for the ministry while attending Harvard University in 1886, probably the last thing Wallace Nutting ever envisioned was a career as a photographer...author...publisher... lecturer...collector...furniture maker...or becoming America's foremost authority on antiques.

But that is exactly what life had in store for this versatile and most gifted individual.

Wallace Nutting was born in 1861 in Rockbottom, Massachusetts. Upon his father's death during the Civil War in 1864, he moved to Maine to live with his grandparents. After working on his grandfather's farm and attending high school there, he entered Exeter Acadamy in 1880. From 1883-1886 he attended Harvard University and from 1886-1888 he attended the Hartford (Connecticut) Theological Seminary and the Union Seminary in New York.

In 1889, Wallace Nutting was ordained as a Congregational minister at the Park Congregational Church in St. Paul, Minnesota. There was no doubt that he always wanted to become a minister as he was frequently quoted as saying "I would rather preach than anything else on earth".

And preach he did. Never willing to acccept second best, Wallace Nutting worked unrelentingly at writing the perfect sermon. He would work many days writing each sermon, and would be tired long afterward.

While they were living in Providence, Rhode Island, his wife,

The China Cupboard, a typical Wallace Nutting "Interior" scene. Nutting Interiors usually featured women in Colonial settings.

Mariet Griswold Nutting, had suggested that he take long bicycle rides into the countryside on Mondays, no doubt to relax from the stress he had incurred preparing for his Sunday sermons. He seemed to feel that if he would take his camera along, the trip would become shorter and more fruitful.

As the next several years went by, he began touring the New England countryside while on vacation, either by carriage, car, or train, taking photographs of rural America. Nutting was one of the first to recognize that the American scene was rapidly changing. Industrialization was altering the way America looked and our pure and picturesque country would never look the same again. He seemed to feel it his divine calling to record the beauty of America for future generations.

Perhaps he worked too hard because his sixteen years in the pulpit began to take its toll. Some sources report that he suffered from vertigo. Others say that he suffered a nervous breakdown resulting from the energy he expended preaching. Regardless of the cause, Wallace Nutting retired from the Ministry in 1904 due to his ill health.

*****

Nutting opened his first studio in New York City in 1904 almost immediately after his retirement but apparently the big-city atmosphere didn't agree with him. After a lengthy illness, he decided that he needed the fresh air of the country. In 1905 he purchased a pre-revolutionary home in Southbury, Connecticut which he named **Nuttinghame**, and opened a larger studio there.

Nutting developed a keen eye for composition and he mastered the technical skills of printing high quality pictures on a special platinum paper. He enhanced the beauty of his pictures by having them hand-colored by a small group of colorists he employed in his studio. He placed some of his pictures in several smaller art and gift shops where they began to readily sell. He then used his early profits to purchase better equipment and to expand the scope of his operations.

Starting first in Vermont, and then eventually traveling throughout the rest of New England, Nutting would photograph country lanes, streams, orchards, lakes, and mountains. Wallace Nutting would take the photograph, assign a title, and instruct his colorists how it should be colored. Each picture that met Nutting's high standards of color, composition, and taste would be affixed to its matting and signed by his employees with the **Wallace Nutting** name. Those pictures that did not meet his strict standards were destroyed.

Beginning first with outdoor scenes in New England, Nutting eventually traveled throughout the United States and Europe, taking photographs in 26 states and 17 foreign countries between 1900-1935. Overall, he took more than 50,000 pictures, 10,000 of which he felt met his high standards. The balance were destroyed.

It was around 1905 that Nutting began taking his first Interior pictures. Supposedly one day while it was raining outside, Mrs Nutting suggested that he take a more 'personable' picture indoors. So he set up a colonial scene in his Southbury home, had an employee dress up in a colonial fashion, and took several different pictures. These sold relatively easily which encouraged him to expand further into this area.

Working in Southbury from 1905-1912, and then in Framingham from 1912 until his death in 1941, Nutting sold literally millions of his hand-colored photographs. Sold throughout the first quarter of the 20th century, well before the invention of color photography, these pictures initially cost only pennies. His picture market was primarily those middle and lower middle class households which could not afford finer forms of art. Because of their low price, Wallace Nutting pictures were purchased in large numbers. By 1925, hardly an American middle-class household was without one. They were purchased as gifts for weddings, showers, Christmas, birthdays, and just about any other reason imaginable.

The height of Wallace Nutting picture popularity was 1915-25. During this time Nutting employed nearly 100 colorists, along with another 100 employees who acted as framers, matters, salesmen, management, and assorted administrative office personnel.

Let there be no mistake about it...Wallace Nutting pictures were big business. Shortly before World War I, the business was grossing as much as a thousand dollars a day.

Up at the Vilas Farm (1912)

Old New England Pictures (1913)

Chapter 2

Wallace Nutting...The Author

Best known among the general public for his hand-colored pictures, Wallace Nutting was also widely recognized as one of the leading authors of his time. He personally authored 19 books, contributed photographs to several other books, published many picture and furniture catalogs, and wrote numerous magazine articles about antiques and colonial living.

Some of Nutting's earliest photographs were first published in 1905. During the previous year he sailed on a cruise through the bible lands along with a large group of ministers, missionaries, and other religious individuals. One result of this trip was the publication of the book **The Cruise of the Eight Hundred To and Through Palestine.** Although Wallace Nutting himself didn't write or publish this book, he did contribute many of the pictures included throughout its nearly 400 pages.

Over the years Nutting contributed photographs to several other books that he did not write, including **Social Life in Old New England** and **Pathway of the Puritans.**

In 1912, Wallace Nutting put together a leather-bound book entitled **Up at the Vilas Farm** for his friend, Charles Nathaniel Vilas. Apparently Mr. Vilas, a wealthy businessman from Alstead, NH, commissioned Nutting to photograph a series of pictures throughout his estate, have them hand-colored, and included in a book which Mr. Vilas gave as gifts to several of his friends or clients.

Up at the Vilas Farm did not include actual copy, but it did have a leather cover, and more than twenty individual pages, each containing a hand-colored photograph, mounted and signed upon an indented, mat-like page. I am aware of only three existing copies of this book.

Nutting's **States Beautiful** Series was published in 2 Editions.
1st Editions (1922-1930) had green covers;
2nd Editions (1935-1937) had tan covers.

It was this book that apparently inspired Nutting to *publish* his first book the following year...**Old New England Pictures.** This book was similar to the **Up at the Vilas Farm** book in that it included 30+ pages of hand-colored pictures, each mounted upon a signed mat-like page. But taking this endeavor several steps further, Nutting added titles to each of the pictures, and more importantly, he included 64 pages of copy on old New England houses. This was his first copyrighted book (1913).

He was more widely known for his '**States Beautiful**' series. As Wallace Nutting traveled throughout America taking his photographs, he wrote eight books about states that he visited. Each book contained approximately 300 of his pictures which had been photographed throughout the state, and copy about the state's key regions and its houses, history, people, and charm.

These books had 2 primary markets. First, the residents of each particular state. Most people like reading about themselves, or at least about something near and dear to them...their home state. As a result, he would sell a considerable number of books to residents of each state that he wrote about.

Secondly, this was an era before travel became inexpensive and convenient. Commercial air travel had not yet arrived, transatlantic ocean voyages were lengthy and expensive, and the automobile was still being perfected. Books were the easiest way to travel. Libraries were frequent purchasers of his **States Beautiful** books, as well as those individuals interested in learning about new and far-away places.

Overall, Nutting published 10 **States Beautiful** books:

> **Vermont Beautiful** (1922, 1936)
> **Massachusetts Beautiful** (1923, 1935)
> **Connecticut Beautiful** (1923, 1937)
> **New Hampshire Beautiful** (1923, 1935)
> **Maine Beautiful** (1924, 1935)
> **Pennsylvania Beautiful** (1924, 1935)
> **Ireland Beautiful** (1925, 1935)
> **New York Beautiful** (1927, 1936)
> **England Beautiful** (1928, 1936)
> **Virginia Beautiful** (1930, 1935)

This **States Beautiful** series also included two books on European countries, England and Ireland, using pictures taken on several of his trips overseas.

Five other **States Beautiful** books were under consideration: Ohio, Colorado, California, New Jersey, and Florida, but none of these were ever published. The dust jacket of the 1st edition **Connecticut Beautiful** book went so far as to state that **Florida Beautiful** was released in 1924 but that apparently never occurred. Twenty-five pages of the unpublished manuscript were found, but no such book was ever published.

Nutting sold many **States Beautiful** books. Based upon comments in **Wallace Nutting's Biography** (Wallace Nutting wrote and published his own biography in 1936), approximately 10,000 copies of most 1st editions were sold. 2nd Editions were released in the mid 1930's.

The success of the **States Beautiful** books led Nutting to publish several other books on subjects where he possessed significant knowledge: clocks and photography. In 1924, he published one of the most definitive books ever written on the subject of clocks...**The Clock Book**. This book pictured nearly 250 clocks, described in detail many forms and variations of different types of clocks, and compiled the most extensive listing of American clock makers known at that time.

Photographic Art Secrets was published in 1927, and included Nutting's philosophy and knowledge of successful photography. Chapters included such diverse topics as **The Tripod, The Shutter, Exposure, Composition, Latitute From The Equator, Animal Pictures,** and much more. For serious picture collectors, this book is a must because it contains many pictures that were never published in any of his States Beautiful books or picture catalogs.

With all of his numerous publications over the years, Nutting published many of his books through his own publishing company, the **Old America Company.** Other books were published by Dodd, Mead & Company, and Marshall, Jones and Company. Later editions were published by Garden City Publishing Company, MacMillan Publishing Company, and Bonanza Books, Inc.

If Wallace Nutting became well-known for his **States Beautiful** series, he became even more famous for the books he published on his true passion: early American antiques.

Nutting claimed that the search for attractive backgrounds for his Interior pictures was responsible for his fascination with antiques. Through the accumulation of antiques for his Interior scenes and for several of his homes, Wallace Nutting had the opportunity to see such a diverse assortment and large quantity of antiques that he began to record what he saw...through his camera.

It was in 1917 that he published his first book on antique furniture...**American Windsors.** Although many antique collectors are aware of Charles Santore's recent publication of two excellent

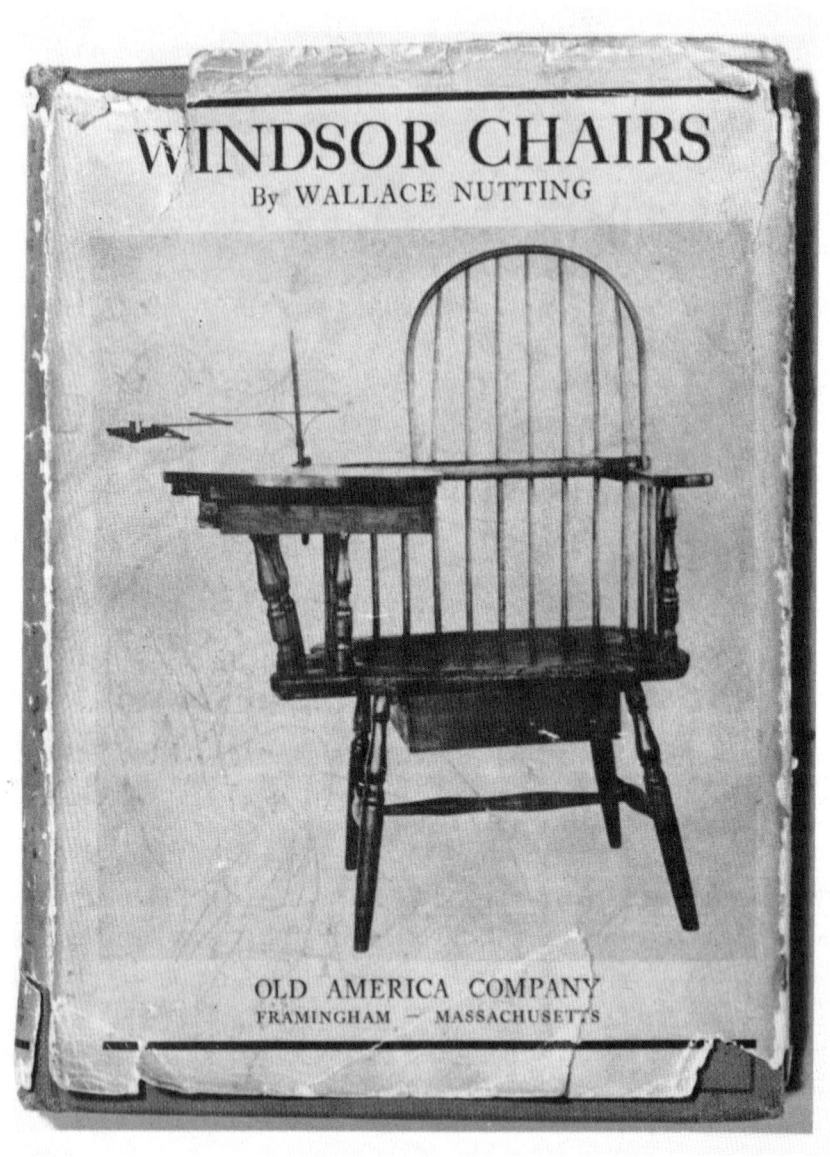

Wallace Nutting published the first comprehensive book on Windsor chairs in 1917.

volumes on Windsor chairs, relatively few are aware that Wallace Nutting wrote the first comprehensive book on Windsor chairs more than 70 years ago...**American Windsors** (the dust jacket called the book **Windsor Chairs**). Nearly 200 pages long, this book was the first serious study of the Windsor form with chairs dating from 1725-1825. Picturing nearly 100 different Windsors, this book included an in-depth discussion of Windsor variations, and each chair's merit, dating, and frequency of occurrence.

Nutting's passion for antiques then led to his publication in 1921 of **Furniture of the Pilgrim Century.** This work went beyond the Windsor form to include American chests, desks, tables, non-Windsor chairs, mirrors, clocks, utensils, and hardware.

Nutting felt that World War I stirred a great deal of patriotism and stimulated interest in the work of our forefathers. Some credit him with playing a significant role in the Colonial Revival Movement. More than 500 pages long, and including more than 1000 photos of items dating between 1620-1720, Wallace Nutting tried to include only things made in America...of native American woods.

In 1924, **The Furniture of the Pilgrim Century** was revised, eliminating some pieces which had been later determined to be of non-American origin, adding a few new sections, and eliminating a few controversial pages on Ironwork.

Wallace Nutting took most of the photos used in this book, and wrote all copy. Except for the more serious collectors, this extensive publication was all but forgotten because it was eclipsed by his most important work...**The Furniture Treasury.**

The Furniture Treasury, still available in bookstores today, is really not one book, but three separate volumes. Volumes I & II, published in 1928, contained more than **5000 photos** of American

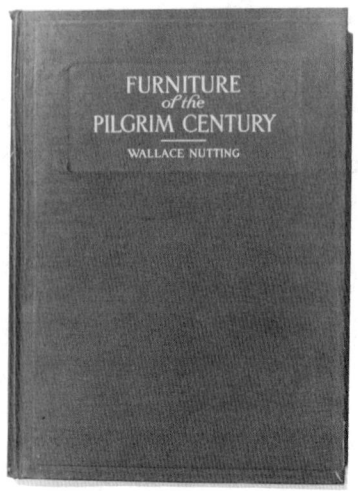

Furniture of the Pilgrim Century (1921)

Furniture Treasury (Vol. I & II, 1928; Vol. III, 1933)

furniture and utensils. Somewhat overlapping the **Furniture of the Pilgrim Century,** this work covers 1650 to the end of the Empire Period which, according to Nutting, *'brings us to the beginning of the degraded styles'.*

In 1933, Nutting published a 3rd volume of **The Furniture Treasury.** Intended as a supplement to Volumes I & II, this book supplied additional details concerning styles, dates, construction, and origins of the previous volumes. It also provided a listing of early American Clock Makers which supplemented the listing in his 1924 publication of **The Clock Book.** Unlike the first two volumes of **The Furniture Treasury,** Volume III had no photographs. Rather, it was illustrated with hundreds of sketches, mostly drawn by his assistant, Ernest John Donnelly.

After more than 60 years in print, **The Furniture Treasury** still has not been superseded as the finest and most complete visual reference book of early American antiques ever published.

With his picture business successfully up and running, and with his interest in the Colonial Revival Movement growing, Nutting started to become more actively involved with antiques. Fortunately for him, he began collecting in an era when many fine early pieces were still available...if one looked hard enough. With so many great antiques still available...and with so much more to learn...Wallace Nutting began his lifelong quest for antiques.

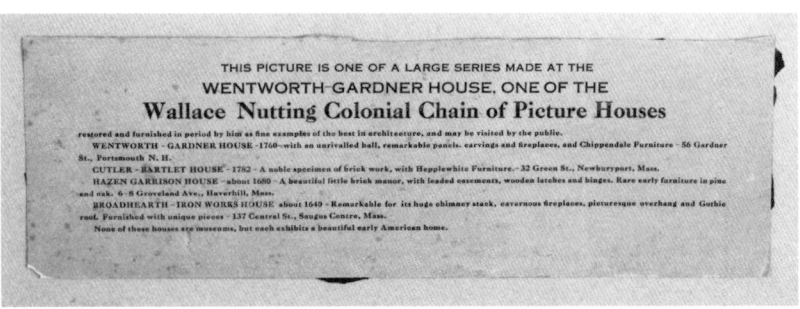

A label from an Interior Scene taken at
the **Wentworth-Gardner House**, Portsmouth, NH,
one of Nutting's **Colonial Chain of Picture Houses**

Chapter 3

Wallace Nutting and Antiques

Although Wallace Nutting began purchasing antiques while in Southbury, he really didn't begin seriously collecting until moving to Framingham.

With the transition from Southbury to Framingham completed in 1912, and with sales of his Interior pictures at an all-time high, Nutting began looking for quaint new settings for his Colonial Interior scenes. Finding the appropriate room with the correct furnishings often proved more difficult than he had anticipated.

He photographed his earliest Interior scenes in his Southbury home...**Nuttinghame.** When he ran out of creative scenes there, he began taking pictures in the homes of his friends. But, as the sale of his Interior scenes began to increase, he felt that new and different settings were needed. So over the next several years, he purchased and restored five historic homes throughout New England.

In 1914, he purchased his first home: the **Wentworth-Gardner House**, 56 Gardner St., Portsmouth, NH. Built in 1760 by Madam Mark Hunking Wentworth, and later owned by Major Gardner of Revolutionary War fame, the house looked out over the Piscataqua River. One of the most important aspects of this house was its upstairs and downstairs hall, once considered the finest hall in America.

Nutting furnished this home with a fine collection of Chippendale mahogany and earlier period furniture worthy of the house. Items included a set of six walnut chairs with rich carvings; a set of fourteen Chippendale chairs, with a three-chair-back settee to match; a specially carved, cabriole-legged, ball and claw bed; a

The Quilting Party, an Interior Scene taken at
the **Wentworth-Gardner House**, Portsmouth, NH

The Interrupted Letter, an Interior Scene taken at
the **Saugus Iron Works (Broadhearth)**, Saugus MA

six-legged highboy; rare gate-legged tables; block front desks; pie crust tables; a set of braced-back Windsors; a 'lounge chaise'; and numerous other pieces of high-style furniture.

This house was built during the period generally considered to be the peak of Georgian style. When Nutting had completed his restoration work, it was furnished just as an American or English gentleman of taste and means would have done during the mid 18th century.

The next home he purchased was the **Hazen "Garrison" House**, 6-8 Groveland Street, Haverhill, MA. Built in 1680, this home was the perfect type of brick English manor house, nearly identical to a home in Kent, England. This house was one of the earliest and most perfectly restored 'Garrison' houses in the country. (Note: A 'Garrison' House was a secured house that settlers retreated to during threat of Indian attack). Furnished with very early pine and oak furniture, this home had several massive fireplaces with double ovens which provided an unusually large provision for cooking. The **Hazen "Garrison" House**, first owned by the Revolutionary War's General Hazen, was said to be the first building used as a shoe factory in America, and was well known for its quaintness, daintiness, and harmony of design.

A third house was the **Cutler-Bartlet House**, 32 Green Street, Newburyport, MA. This was built about 1782 and was the largest home in the chain. Furnished with a variety of Chippendale, Hepplewhite, and Sheraton furniture, individual pieces included secretaries, mahogany tables, sideboards, highboys, lowboys, and a very large collection of Windsor chairs. This particular house was the boyhood home of John Pierrepont, grandfather of the famous J.P. Morgan.

This home was also used as a secondary picture studio during the summer months, allowing tourists to watch as colorists tinted the 'famous' Wallace Nutting pictures. Many Wallace Nutting pictures hung throughout the house, many beside older historical prints.

The **Iron Works House,** or **Broadhearth,** 127 Center Street, Saugus, MA was purchased in 1916. This was the site of the first working iron works in the colonies in 1642. It still possessed the bog pits where early iron was dug and had a working foundry where Nutting began a brief business in reproduction ironwork. This house was the oldest in Saugus, one of the oldest in the country, and one of the few early houses where the overhang appeared on the side, showing a strong Gothic influence. The early furniture, with many pieces dating from the 1600's included trestle tables, pilgrim chairs, and oak chests. The house included several massive fireplaces which were said to be some of the largest in the country, and which were featured in many of his Interior scenes.

The **Webb House,** or **Hospitality Hall,** 89 Main Street, Wethersfield, CT, was purchased in 1916, featured Dutch and Chippendale furniture, and was built in 1752. Much of the beauty in Webb House was centered around rooms with beautifully colored wallpaper.

Nutting purchased these five homes because he felt each represented a different period of early American style and architecture. Hoping to capitalize on the growing motor-tourist trade, they were completely restored and refurbished, and then opened to the public for a small admission fee, coming to be known as **The Wallace Nutting Colonial Chain of Picture Houses**

By 1920, all had been sold. Three of the houses (Wentworth-Gardner House, Cutler-Bartlet House, and Webb House), and their entire contents, were sold to **John Wanamaker's** Department Store. The antiques were exhibited by Wanamaker's in New York before being publically sold, while the houses were sold in separate transactions.

The two remaining homes (Saugus Iron Works and the Hazen-Garrison House) were sold privately, while their contents were sold to an antique dealer, presumably for inventory.

Nutting claims to have made neither a profit nor loss on the sale of his Colonial Chain of Houses. *"Some houses were sold at a fraction of cost, others far above cost, but the average was a stalemate".*

But it was in this period, 1914-20, that Wallace Nutting began his close association with antiques. An education in antiques has never been easy to come by, especially in those days. Compared to today, there were very few reference books in print, and even fewer places to turn for advice. Most of his education was a self-learning process. He read whatever books were available, toured museums and private collections, and visited with individuals more scholarly and knowledgeable than himself. He attended auctions, visited a variety of dealers, and was even known to knock on a stranger's door asking to preview their antiques.

For someone with the high moral fiber of a minister, Nutting was not always totally above-board in trying to achieve his goals and objectives in his pursuit of antiques. According to one researcher... *"Nutting was a buccaneer of a collector. Lacking a fortune with which to buy antiques, he wheedled, conspired, sermonized, and all but promised salvation to get the antique that he wanted. He argued that the owner of a fine antique without the means to properly protect or display it had a moral obligation to turn it over to someone who could - namely Wallace Nutting".*

A Stately Tea Pouring, taken at **Webb House,** Wethersfield, CT, another home in the Colonial Chain

A Virginia Reel, taken at **Nuttingholme,** his home in Framingham, MA

One such story centers around his purchase of the famous Prence-Howes Court Cupboard. Nutting had purchased this court cupboard in 1921 from an Abby Howes, a Danvers, Massachusetts school teacher, for $3000. Apparently this piece had been in her family for generations, had once been owned by the first governor of the Pilgrim Colony, but Nutting somehow succeeded in convincing Mrs. Howe to sell it to him.

Upon learning that Nutting was going to resell that court cupboard to J.P. Morgan for **$20,000** as part of his personal antique collection, Mrs, Howe sued to regain her family heirloom, claiming that: 1) Nutting persuaded her that it was her civic duty to sell it to him 2) That he told her he planned to put the cupboard on display at his Framingham Studio where others could study and appreciate it 3) That Nutting promised to hire her as his secretary so that she could continue to be close to her cupboard (he never did) 4) That he assured her that his offer was a fair one and that the cupboard was worth no more than what he offered.

Nutting's defense was that the court cupboard was indeed worth no more than $3000 when he had purchased it. But **his** ownership of it, along with the added-value now attached to it resulting from its association with the respected Wallace Nutting name, had increased its value to the present level.

Nutting testified that he had almost sold his antique collection to Henry Ford, but, after further negotiations, decided to sell his collection to J.P. Morgan. *"Morgan didn't know any more about an antique cupboard than a hole in the wall"* Nutting testified under oath.

Nutting won the case, and the cupboard is now part of the Wallace Nutting Collection residing in the Wadsworth Atheneum in Hartford, Connecticut.

Nutting claims that he experienced three distinct phases in his antique collecting career.

Phase I began with the furnishing of his houses...Nuttinghame, Nuttingholme, and the five houses in his Colonial Chain. This was his basic learning phase and resulted in many mistakes which undoubtedly added to his overall knowledge.

In order to completely furnish these seven houses, Nutting purchased well over a thousand antiques during this phase, and rejected many thousands of others.

Initially Nutting only appreciated the earliest forms, that is, Pilgrim, William & Mary, Windsor chairs, and a few other 17th century forms. But it was during this period that Nutting first began to appreciate some of the "later styles", i.e., Queen Anne, Chippendale, Hepplewhite, and Sheraton. This phase of collecting ended upon the sale of his Colonial Chain in 1920.

Phase II began shortly after he sold his picture and furniture business in 1922 for somewhere around $120,000. Upon entering his second 'retirement', he began a much more serious period of antique collecting and accumulation, using much of the proceeds obtained from the sale of his business during this phase. This was his most serious and dedicated phase of collecting during which he was able to accumulate the majority of what eventually came to be known as **The Wallace Nutting Collection of Early American Antiques**. This phase ended with the sale of his personal antique collection to J.P. Morgan in 1923.

Phase III was a more informal, low-key collecting phase, consisting of what he termed "odd buying", purchasing items for use in his home, items to copy in his reproduction business, or things that he simply liked and presumed would end up as part of his estate after his death.

During his years of collecting, Nutting developed a series of rules for buying antiques, some of which included:

> *1) Buy only good things in fair condition. Things repaired are little better, or worse than new.*
> *2) Buy not for age only, but for beauty, or merit, or use, or rarity. Two of these reasons ought always to inhere in the articles.*
> *3) Buy only after taste is cultivated by reading the books on the subject, of course Wallace Nutting books!*
> *4) Buy only with good advice - not a dealer's advice. Are you looking for men to be angels before their time?*
> *5) Buy only for a specific place in the dwelling. Get something you need, not something that is merely a bargain.*
> *6) Do not collect one class of articles, but a variety. They who collect a class should found a museum.*
> *7) Buy mostly American articles because they look well in an American setting.*
> *8) Never collect "fixed up" furniture. That means passing by many shops entirely. It is usually impossible for an expert to detect, on a nice piece of work, where the new begins.*
> *9) Collect what you learn to be approved after many years' trial as to style. Do not buy merely because you like it.*

These guidelines for buying antiques seem nearly as applicable today as they did when Nutting first published them more than 50 years ago.

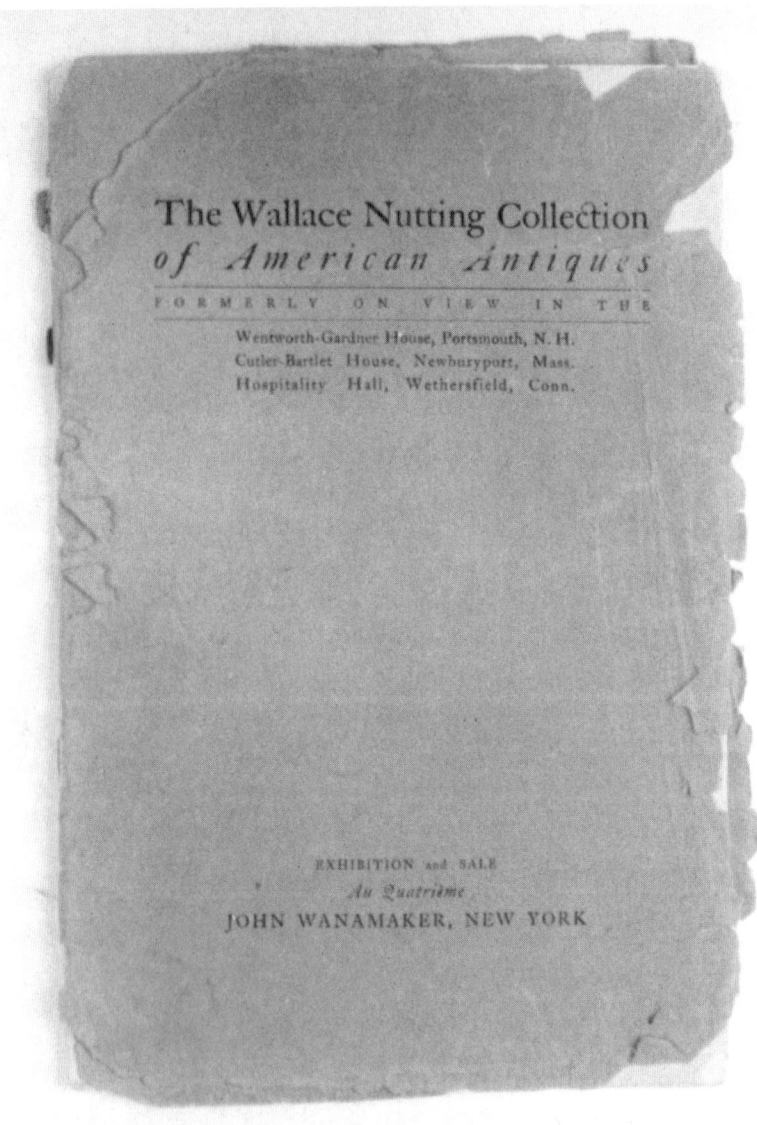

John Wanamaker's Catalog for the Exhibition and Sale
of the contents of three Colonial Chain Homes

Nutting's antique education obviously was accelerated due to the incredibly large number of pieces he found. While researching his antique books, he came into contact with well over 20,000 different antiques. The better ones were photographed and included in his books; the remainder were studied for their bad points. Nothing was lost in his quest for knowledge.

Over the years, Nutting's vast experience with antiques led him to become a recognized expert on the subject. Perhaps he wasn't considered the most scholarly or knowledgeable man in his field but he did become the most widely known. He contributed numerous articles to such respected publications as **The Magazine Antiques, The Saturday Evening Post**, and **Women's World**. He gave lectures, provided slide presentations, and was consulted by some of the top scholars and wealthiest collectors in the country.

In what really amounted to only a few years, Nutting became one of the country's leading authorities on antiques.

But it was during Nutting's earliest phase of collecting that he realized a very important point: Even as early as 1917, with many other people actively collecting early American antiques, frequently the finest examples were unobtainable.

Being the entrepreneur that he was, he quickly realized that if he was having difficulty obtaining the finest forms of early American antiques, so too were other collectors. Many could not afford the finest forms and, quite often, those who could afford them could not find them.

It was his love of antiques...and his uncanny sense of entrepreneurial spirit...that led Wallace Nutting to his least profitable, and according to some, most important business venture of all. It was at this point, beginning in 1917, that Wallace Nutting decided to begin reproducing furniture.

Wallace Nutting Windsors...Correct Windsor Furniture
Nutting's first furniture catalog was published in 1918

Chapter 4

Wallace Nutting Windsor Chairs

As mentioned earlier, Wallace Nutting completed the first definitive study on Windsor chairs with the publication of **American Windsors** in 1917. In researching this book Nutting sought out the finest Windsor forms he could find, assembling a collection of nearly 150 chairs. Approximately 75% of the chairs photographed for this book were owned by Nutting himself.

It therefore shouldn't come as any surprise that the first furniture Nutting began reproducing was Windsor chairs. Nor is it too surprising that Nutting released his first Reproduction Furniture Catalog, **Wallace Nutting Windsors...Correct Windsor Furniture** in 1918, shortly after the publication of **American Windsors**. After all, timing is everything in business and what better time to begin selling reproduction Windsor chairs than at the same time a new book on Windsor chairs is released. His Windsor Chair Catalog contained some superb examples... which were unavailable anywhere else...except through Wallace Nutting's furniture company.

This chapter will focus specifically on the production of Windsor chairs and other furniture using the Windsor form. Considerable time will be spent discussing Windsors because it is far and away the most common type of Wallace Nutting furniture you will find. Also, many of the construction and finishing procedures that apply to Windsor chairs were used upon his other types of furniture as well.

A later chapter will focus upon other forms of Wallace Nutting furniture.

A Wallace Nutting Knuckle Arm Comb Back Windsor
New England Turnings...#415

* * * * *

Wallace Nutting started reproducing furniture in 1917 at an old woolen mill called the Scott Mill. This site was adjacent to the Saugus Iron Works property which he had just recently purchased and restored as part of his Colonial Chain.

Nutting had long felt that the Windsor form was one of the finest styles of furniture ever produced in Colonial America...and one of the most abused forms as well. Many had tried to reproduce Windsors before him but, in his opinion, no one had yet done it correctly. He seemed to consider it his divine calling to resurrect the Windsor chair. His 1918 Windsor Chair Catalog begins with this bold statement: *The Redemption of the Windsor Chair: All persons of taste and discernment will be glad that at last someone has had the courage to undertake the redemption of the Windsor Chair.*

Since he owned nearly 150 different examples of Windsor chairs, Nutting had ample opportunity to study the best...and worst...examples of Windsor design. Out of his huge collection of Windsors, Nutting claimed to have found only **one** (his #310) perfect enough to reproduce **exactly**. By placing such a large grouping of chairs together, Nutting felt that nearly all fell short in some respect of what he perceived to be the "perfect" Windsor Chair. If the comb was just right, the legs were too short; if the seat was nearly perfect, the back was not; if the height was correct, the woods were incorrect. Practically no chair he found ever lived up to his concept of the "perfect" Windsor chair.

With so few original Windsors meeting his high standards, Nutting set out to *create* the perfect Windsor chair, with every part suggesting grace, strength, harmony, and comfort. If the grandest 18th century craftmen were unable to produce the "perfect" Windsor, then Wallace Nutting would do it himself.

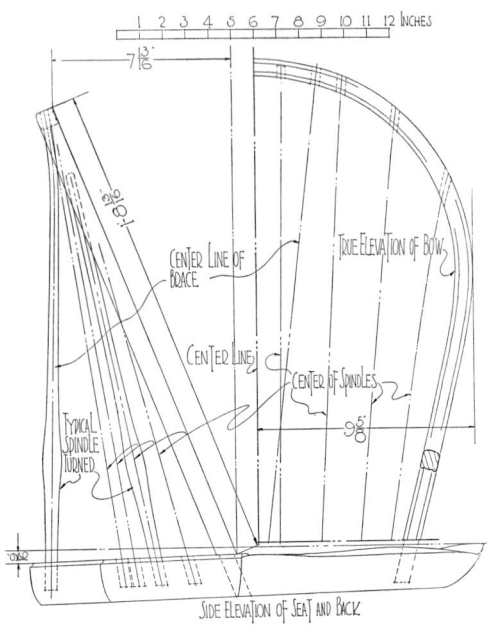

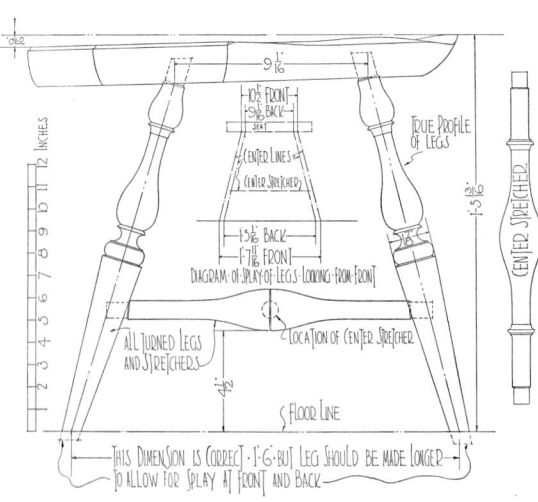

Windsor Chair Drawings

In order to produce the "perfect" Windsor chair, correct in every detail, Nutting would generally follow a 5-step approach:

1) Observation and Analysis. The first step in copying a piece of furniture would be to closely study and analyze it. Nutting, with the help of the craftsmen he employed, would visually inspect a chair from all sides. They would look at the piece's overall merit and compare it to other fine Windsors. Where appropriate, photographs were taken. Each dimension was carefully recorded and when necessary, an entire chair would be carefully taken apart, measured inch-for-inch, turn-for-turn...until Nutting understood what made the chair so correct and appealing.

2) Detailed Sketches and Drawings. Once a piece was selected for reproduction, many scaled drawings were made: frontal views, side views, rear views, top views, and bottom views. Each drawing would include the exact dimensions of each component part, down to the 1/16 of an inch.

3) Adjustments and Improvements. Since most chairs Nutting selected for reproduction were *nearly* "perfect", most characteristics were already "correct". Nutting would focus upon those few aspects that still needed to be *"corrected"* in order to make the chair "perfect", describing in detail what adjustments were needed to the chair's dimensions, design, turnings, or woods.

4) Patterns. Once Nutting's "improvements" were made and the final scale drawings completed, a chair was nearly ready for production. The next step was to construct **paper patterns** for each individual component in the chair, with a separate pattern being created for the seat, legs, stretchers, spindles, bows, and arms.

For items which were to be reproduced frequently over a longer period of time, **wooden patterns** were constructed.

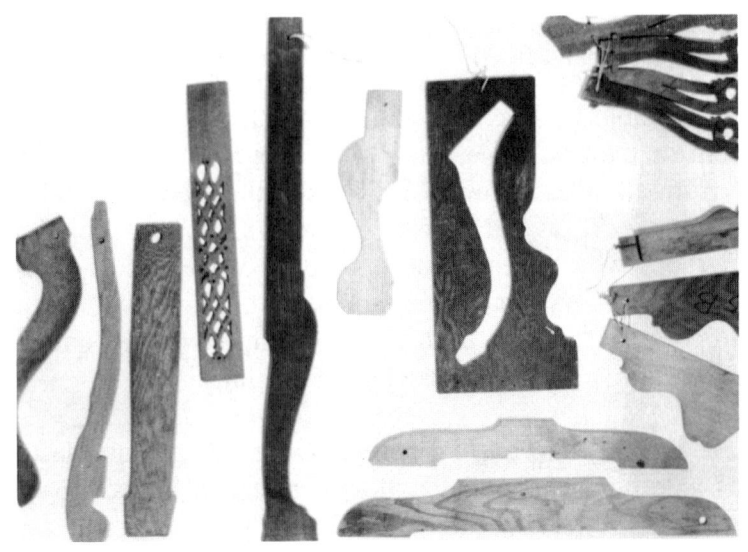

Wallace Nutting Wooden Furniture Patterns

Wallace Nutting Model Furniture Pieces

5) Model Pieces of Furniture. Finally, sample pieces of each individual component were constructed by closely following the patterns. Once these individual 'Model' components met with Nutting's approval, an entire chair was assembled using individual Model pieces. Once the entire chair was correct, this became the final Model Chair that was to be followed as closely as possible by the workmen, without deviation.

Windsor Chair Construction

The key to the inherent beauty of any piece of furniture lies in its construction...those special production techniques which are nearly invisible to all but the master craftsmen. Through his close analysis and observation, Nutting took note of those special techniques and included those that he felt necessary to create his perfect Windsor.

Nutting felt he could produce a chair for one-twentieth the cost by machine, but a machine-produced chair nearly as good as one made by hand was a chair *"degraded to the capacity of the machines"*. As a result, his Windsor chairs were created entirely by hand.

Seats

Each seat was shaped from a **single piece of Country Pine 2" thick**. After being cut to the desired shape, the center of the seat was deeply scooped to nearly one-half the thickness (1"), and at the edges the chamfer was shaped above and below to meet in a hairline, giving the impression of a much lighter, thinner, and more delicate seat.

Any tailpieces were also hand-finished, with a hollow, half-round molding completing the back of the seat.

With all the hand-work involved, a normal craftsman was capable of completing only three or four seats per day.

WN Windsors are generally 18" from seat top to floor in front, and 17 1/2" from seat top to floor in rear.

The Rake, or Splay, is 4"

Legs, Stretchers, and Spindles

All legs and stretchers were finished on a hand-lathe. Although Nutting felt that a machine could produce a decent turning at considerable savings, he sincerely believed that machines had to be avoided because they could not provide the extremely deep cuts or delicate lines needed for the correct look. The bulbs were a full 2" and the tapered legs were turned to 3/4" or 7/8".

Once the legs were attached to the seat, seats were precisely 18" from seat top-to-floor in the front, and one-half inch shorter (17 1/2") in the rear. Two exceptions to the 18" rule were Slipper chairs (15") and Child's chairs (10").

All legs were raked 4" within 18" in order to provide the greatest strength and stability.

Wherever the legs entered the thinned portion of the seat, they generally penetrated the seat entirely, wedged from the top in their grooved joint.

All spindles were one piece, running through any arm rails and bows to the top of the chair, penetrating the bow or hoop back, except on the sides. At least three spindles were pinned and all were glued. The bracing spindles were pinned top and bottom.

Bows, Combs, and Arms

Bow backs entirely penetrated the seat from above, and were wedged from below the seat. Because of their excessive length, they were carved entirely by hand rather than machine, and were bent using wet steam.

All combs were delicately shaped and thinned from the lower to the upper edge, entirely by hand, giving them an added feel of

A Wallace Nutting Knuckle Arm Bow Back Windsor
New England Turnings...#420

delicacy and lightness, and bent using wet steam. Combs were pinned in at least three places, and glued to each spindle.

All assembling was done with fox-tail wedges and hot glue.

Arm rails, where ending in a knuckle, were carved entirely by hand, and were 1/2" nearer the seat in the front than in the back.

The point I am trying to impress upon you is that **each** of these steps contributed to a finer, more correct Windsor chair. None of these procedures were 'discovered' by Nutting. Each step had been known by furniture makers since the 18th century.

But the difference is that **each additional step takes more time…and costs more money.** Most furniture makers over the years were willing to cut a few corners, produce each chair just a little faster, thereby shaving their costs as much as possible. The end result was inevitably an inferior chair.

The difference between a Wallace Nutting Windsor Chair and Windsor chairs from other furniture makers is that **Wallace Nutting didn't cut corners. He produced each chair as well as it could be constructed, regardless of expense.**

Windsor Chair Woods

Generally Wallace Nutting Windsors were made of three different woods: **Rock Maple** for the legs; **Country Pine** for the seats; and **Hickory** for the spindles, bows, bent-arm rails, and combs.

According to Nutting's 1918 Windsor Chair Catalog:

"Maple is the most generally useful of furniture woods. It soon took the place of oak and beech. It was abundant, strong, often very

A Wallace Nutting Windsor Candlestand
New England Turnings...#17

handsome, smooth working, and freer from the worm than most woods. Further there is much fine American sentiment in connection with the rock (what a strong name) maple, otherwise called the sugar maple. A tree which furnished its sweetness for many a year, of a flavor unsurpassed - the natural and uncultivated source of all the sugar needed, was later cut down and worked into furniture and kept on in a useful career. It made the best hot fire. It was the American wood above all.

Pine was a wonderfully useful wood, rare in parts of the world from which our ancestors came. The great 'pumpkin' pines supplied wall panels up to four feet in width. It cut like cheese, but was very durable and pleasantly aromatic. The merits of unfinished pine, its rich, soft yellow browns have not been felt sufficiently. People hasten to cover it with paint. The seat of a windsor was made of knotty pine which would not split and was therefore valuable. It went well with maple.

Hickory became the reliance of the settler for all work requiring toughness and lightness. Spindles and spokes were perfect for this wood."

Turning Variations

The most common turning used in Nutting Windsors was the **"Northern"** or **"New England"** turning. The most obvious characteristics of this style included the straight tapered leg and the bulbous spindles.

Northern or **New England** turnings account for approximately 85% of the Wallace Nutting Windsor Chairs you will find.

The **"Pennsylvania"** or **"Philadelphia"** Windsor was actually an earlier Windsor form, but is much rarer in Wallace Nutting

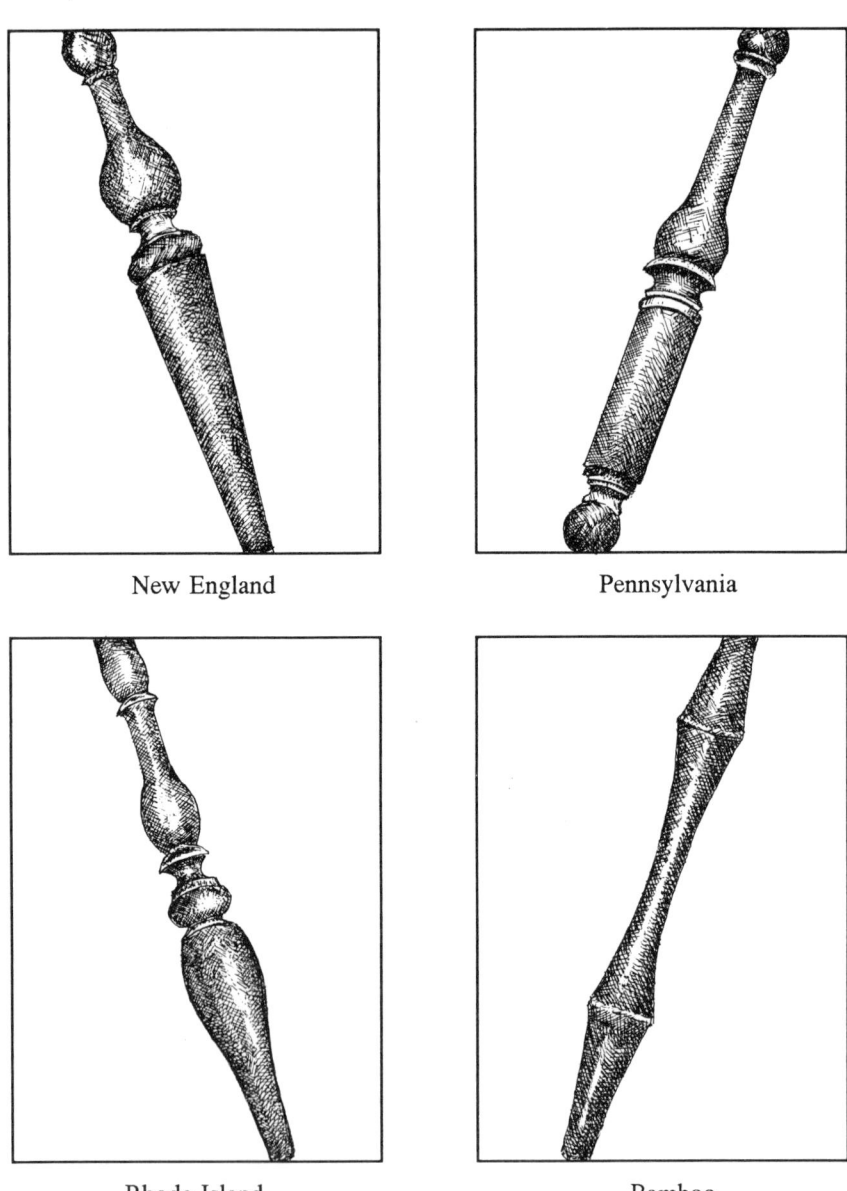

Four Types of Wallace Nutting Turnings

furniture. The primary characteristic of the **Pennsylvania** turnings focus upon the cylinder and ball foot legs, and the straight taper spindles.

Whereas the **New England** spindle had a simple bulbous turning approximately 6" above the seat, flowing into a gradual taper as it entered the bow or comb, the **Pennsylvania** spindle contained no bulbous turning. Rather, it simply flowed from its thickest point where it left the seat, gradually thinning until it entered the rail and comb.

Pennsylvania turnings account for approximately 10% of the Wallace Nutting Windsor Chairs you will find, making them **significantly rarer** than the **New England** variation.

Two additional turnings Nutting produced were the **Rhode Island** turning and the **Bamboo** turning. The **Rhode Island** type had a hollowed taper foot, slightly bowed at the top of the taper. The latest Windsor form that Nutting copied was the **Bamboo** turning.

Sales on both were quite low, with combined production for both forms accounting for less than 5% of the Nutting Windsors you will find.

Nutting stopped reproducing Windsor chairs with the **Bamboo** turning. He felt that Sheraton Windsors, which dated approximately 1800-1810, were the beginning of the degraded Windsor form.

Windsor Chair Finishes

The greatest chair, with a mediocre finish, becomes an average piece of furniture. After going to such great lengths to produce such a fine piece of furniture, the detail-oriented Nutting was not about to degrade the end result of his work with a cheap finish.

Each part of every chair he produced was finished at least five times by hand, usually with a special shellac finish with hand rubbings between each coat. The cost of Nutting's finishing alone exceeded the total cost of most other manufacturer's reproductions. His refinishers were only able to turn out three chairs per day, on a good day.

Overall, the vast majority of Nutting Windsors, perhaps 98-99%, were finished in only two styles, a darker "antique" or mahogany finish, or in a lighter maple, or amber, finish. Of these two styles I would say that the breakdown would be approximately 50-50.

Of the darker mahogany finish, Nutting said *"It has the merit that a chair so finished will never require doing over. The older it grows the more the natural wear will blend with the finish, and the richer and softer will the surface become."*

In all my years of collecting, I have rarely seen a Wallace Nutting chair finished in his *original* paint. Yet, according to Nutting's sales literature, he did offer several different types of paint. Bottle Green, Eggshell Enamel Black, Old Red, and Yellow were all available in 1918.

The rarity of Nutting chairs finished in his original paint can be supported by the recent sale of a matched set of eight green-painted Windsors (6 Braced Bow Back Side Chairs and 2 Knuckle Arm Sack Back Chairs), selling for a Wallace Nutting Auction Record price of **$15,950** at Sotheby's earlier this year.

However, under no circumstances would he sell a chair in **white paint**. (*"In no case will we use white paint, which is an abomination on Windsors, entirely unsuited to their homely, sturdy quality"*.)

Nor would he sell a Windsor painted with more than one color. *("The earliest Windsors in the period were not so painted. That style came only with the degraded Sheraton backs and the rungs which followed round the legs, abandoning the middle stretcher".)*

Markings

Let there be no mistake about it, Wallace Nutting made excellent furniture. And because this furniture was so well made, Nutting wanted it clearly marked so it would unquestionably be identified as **Wallace Nutting Furniture.** The earliest Nutting Windsors were marked with a simple Paper Label. Later pieces were literally **branded** with the Wallace Nutting name.

Chapter 9 will discuss the various markings on Wallace Nutting furniture in much greater detail. Feel free to skip ahead to page 99 if you would like to preview several of the different markings Nutting used. But rather than discussing markings here, the entire subject of identifying Wallace Nutting furniture through its various markings will make much more sense when grouped together into an entire chapter later in this book.

At this point you should simply be aware that Nutting clearly marked most, **but not all**, of his furniture.

Unmarked Windsor Chairs

According to his 1918 Windsor Chair Catalog, Nutting refused to sell anything unfinished... *"We do not care to have our name associated with the bizarre effects sometimes tried on Windsors, and we therefore do not supply chairs 'in the white', that is, unfinished"*.

Apparently he relented on this point in later years because,

WALLACE NUTTING
HIS FURNITURE
MADE BY HIM, ONLY, AT
46 PARK ST., FRAMINGHAM, MASS.
FINISHES

"In the white" {Sold without guarantee} no finish whatever. Name omitted, because of danger of swelling and unsatisfactory finish.

"Natural" A rarely used finish, clear white shellac, on curly maple; used on order only.

"Amber" same as { All maple, oak and pine
"Old Maple"   { in this finish, a light stain followed by many coats of orange shellac, ending with bee's wax. Ornaments and molds on oak are black or maroon.

"Mahogany"   Used only on solid mahogany.

"Walnut" A French walnut used on walnut. Other woods in walnut finish, on order.

"Vandyke Brown" Goes well with mahogany. To order on maple and pine.

"Paint" Black on plain turned chairs is proper, and bottle green, black, old red and yellow on Windsors. To order only.

"Oil" Table tops for dining, or refections, finished in oil regularly, to prevent discoloration.

All special finishes subject to delay.

An Advertising Piece for Wallace Nutting Finishes

according to the advertising piece shown on page 46, he **was** later selling pieces 'in the white', but without guarantee, and with his *"Name omitted, because of danger of swelling and unsatisfactory finish"*.

Nutting also offered to begrudgingly sell unsigned pieces in his 1927-28 Furniture Catalog. On page 3 of that catalog, in a section titled **Unfinished Furniture**, Nutting writes: *"If necessary, but contrary to my advice, pieces not too large will be sold unfinished. But said furniture is liable to sudden swelling. I do not warrant it, and do not care to burn my name on it..."*

Just to make sure you understand the significance of this point, let me rephrase it: **Nutting DID NOT put his name on every single piece of furniture that left his factory. He omitted his name from furniture that was not finished according to his strict refinishing standards.**

Neither his 1930 nor 1937 Furniture Catalogs mention the sale of unsigned, unfinished furniture, but it is unclear whether he simply stopped selling furniture *"in the white"* by this time, or whether he still sold it, but did not advertise it in his catalogs.

Now imagine for a minute what may possibly be sitting in private collections, museums, or circulating through the trade. It's no secret that a good craftsmen or furniture maker can build a brand new piece of furniture, artificially age it, and make it look old. Things are being made **today** that are good enough to fool many experts, let alone the average collector.

Now consider how many Wallace Nutting Windsor Chairs may have been sold *unfinished and unmarked*...**more than 60 years ago**. Chairs that could have been artificially and prematurely aged, painted by someone else, and now having **60 years of wear and patina added to them!** Fifty chairs? One hundred? More? No one really knows because no production records have ever been found.

We do know this:

That in the 1920's, a Nutting Child's High Chair, originally selling for $19 was artificially aged and resold for nearly **$1000...in the 1920's.** It took Wallace Nutting himself, the maker of the furniture, to discover the fraud.

Some years ago it was reported that **Winterthur** removed from exhibition a supposedly 18th century Windsor High Chair after it was suspected of having originated in Nutting's shop.

Supposedly several other **Museums** have quietly removed Nutting pieces as well.

I have personally seen more than two dozen Wallace Nutting Windsors being offered as original at antique shops and shows. How many have I not seen?

In May, 1988 the **Maine Antique Digest** reported a story of a criminal case in New Jersey whereby two individuals sold a Windsor chair to a collector for $6000, claiming it to be an original 18th century piece. The collector eventually came to believe the chair was not as represented and demanded his money back. When the sellers refused to refund the $6000, a lawsuit and trial developed.

At the trial, three experts were called to testify. Each inspected the chair...and all three disagreed.

One expert, a specialist in furniture restoration and handmade American antiques, figured the chair was made about 5-10 years ago, and was worth about $500.

Another expert, a South Jersey auctioneer and appraiser with 22 years experience, thought the chair was worth $3000-$4000, and estimated that the chair was made between 1830-1850, or possibly as late as the 1870's.

The third expert, Charles Santore, A Philadelphia Windsor Chair collector and author of two books on Windsor Chairs, testified that the chair was worth about $1500, was made around 1920-1930, and was a Wallace Nutting reproduction.

(Although I did not personally inspect the chair, based upon the photograph in the **Maine Antique Digest**, there was no doubt in my mind that the chair was a Wallace Nutting, #415, Comb Back Knuckle Arm Chair...and was indeed worth around $1500 today.)

Anyway, the point is this...if Wallace Nutting Reproduction Windsor Chairs are good enough to fool Experts **and** Museums, how many unsigned, unmarked Nutting Windsors are still being cherished by unsuspecting collectors today as authentic, period pieces.

That's a scary throught.

Rarity

With Nutting reproducing over 100 different forms of Windsor chairs between 1917 and 1937, what is considered common, and what is considered rare?

Without any production records, we don't know exactly how many of each form were produced. Nor do we know how many of each form are still in existence today.

Over the past 15 years I have seen a great deal of Wallace Nutting furniture, ranging from single pieces to entire collections. I receive hundreds of letters per year from people asking me to value their

A Wallace Nutting Swivel Windsor
New England Turnings...#329

furniture, I attend numerous shows and auctions, I follow the trade papers religiously, and I've lost count of the number of phone calls I've received from people asking me about their furniture.

As a result of this extensive exposure to Wallace Nutting furniture over the years, I feel comfortable offering these following guidelines regarding the rarity of Wallace Nutting Windsor Chairs:

* Arm chairs are much rarer than side chairs
* Pennsylvania chairs are much rarer than New England chairs
* Rhode Island and Bamboo turnings are rarer than New England and Pennsylvania turnings, but they are also less desirable to most collectors
* Settees, child's chairs, and baby cribs are extremely rare
* Fan Back side chairs are rarer than Bow Back side chairs
* Continuous Arm chairs are rarer than Knuckle Arm chairs
* Windsors with Nutting's *original* paint are **extremely rare**
* The Light Maple Finish and darker Mahogany finishes are both fairly common, with the darker finish being somewhat more desirable to collectors
* 10 Leg Settees are rarer than 6 Leg Settees
* Low Back Windsor chairs are rare, but generally less desirable than higher back Windsors
* Tenoned Arm pieces are rare
* Writing Arm Windsors are quite rare
* Double Combs or Imposed Combs are quite rare

Remember these are only guidelines. But if I were to present one general Rule of Thumb regarding rarity, it would be this:

> **Rule of Thumb...The more difficult a piece was to produce, the higher the original cost. The higher the original cost, the fewer pieces produced, and the rarer they are today.**

One additional thought I want to leave you with is this: **Windsor chairs are the most common type of Wallace Nutting Furniture you will find,** for several reasons.

First, he was producing Windsor chairs longer than his other forms of furniture. Starting in 1917, he continued to manufacture Windsor chairs throughout the 1930's. On the other hand, he only produced his more formal, non-Windsor styles from the mid 1920's, which gave him fewer total productive years.

Secondly, he produced more variations of Windsor chairs than his other forms of furniture, offering more than 100 Windsor designs over his 20 year furniture career. All these forms combined account for a very large percentage of his total production when compared to any other single form (e.g., tables) or style (e.g., Chippendale).

Third, his Windsor chairs were generally less expensive than his other chairs and furniture, which made them more affordable to some people, especially during the 1930 Depression years.

And finally, the Windsor chair has always been a very popular form. Its simplicity in design has made it one of the most desirable forms ever produced and its popularity has held true over the years.

Nutting Windsor chairs were especially popular with professional and business people during the 1920-30's. It was fairly common for banks, doctors, dentists, lawyers, and other professional offices to furnish their waiting rooms and reception areas with Wallace Nutting chairs, thereby contributing to the larger overall production volume.

We are aware of one elderly doctor who furnished his entire waiting room with Wallace Nutting furniture in the 1930's, and used it continually until the 1980's. It was only when he became informed of its current value that he decided to quietly replace it with more contemporary furniture.

*****

In summary, Nutting really didn't copy any single chair *exactly*. Rather, he would take the best examples of the various Windsor forms, copy those characteristics he felt were the best, and incorporate any improvements he felt were needed in order to produce a perfect Windsor chair.

No single feature in any chair is false or inaccurate. Each style of chair, from the simplest Bow Back to the most complex Writing Arm Windsor, contained those features which were indicative of the finest surviving examples of that particular form.

But it was the incorporation of so many correct and wonderful characteristics into a single chair that almost made Nutting Windsors appear to be somewhat of an exaggeration in form.

If there was to be one primary criticism of Nutting Windsors, it would be that his reproductions were **too good**. Their form was **too perfect**...their lines were **too correct**...their overall design was **too good to be true**. I would have to think that if Nutting were alive today, he would have to be pleased with such flattering criticism: **His Windsor chairs were too good.**

I am aware of no other 20th century furniture makers who produced Windsors nearly as good as Nutting, on the scale that Nutting accomplished. Certainly there were other good furniture makers in the early 20th century...and yes, some did produce very nice Windsors...but compared to Nutting, their overall output was miniscule and their impact was minimal.

It was Nutting's initial success in reproducing Windsor chairs, and the early commercial success that followed, that encouraged him to expand into two other endeavors...the reproduction of early American Ironwork...and reproducing other non-Windsor forms of antique furniture.

Chapter 5

Wallace Nutting Ironwork

It was in the restoration of his Chain of Colonial Homes that Nutting first began to understand and appreciate early American Ironwork. The earliest American homes had a great need for products made from iron. The hearth, which was the center of home life, needed the most diverse forms: andirons, shovels, and tongs for working with the fire; cranes, pot hooks, skewers, trivets, and forks, for cooking over the fire.

Lighting fixtures, door latches, door hinges, and window shutter fasteners were all made from iron. Wrought iron nails were used to hold things together, and iron bolts were used for heavier duty fastening work.

Apparently Nutting had great difficulty in locating a good source for early ironwork, correct in detail, and providing the 17th and 18th century look and feel that he needed. Nutting wanted every detail in his Chain of Colonial Homes to be as accurate as possible so, when he couldn't locate a source for the iron that he wanted, he decided to produce it himself.

Wallace Nutting had purchased the Saugus Iron Works for two primary reasons. First, he felt this home was architecturally unique. Not only was it one of the oldest houses in the country, but it also contained much of its original 17th century iron hardware which he felt gave it the finishing touches of originality.

Secondly, this house represented the earliest iron works in America. This had been the residence of America's first successful Iron Master, Joseph Jenks, the inventor of the long scythe. Jenk's invention had enabled the earliest Americans to harvest their crops

Early American Ironwork, 1919 (James Murphey Collection)

three times as quickly as before, thereby symbolizing one of the earliest major improvements to farm productivity in the colonies.

After Nutting refurbished the Iron Master's home to his satisfaction, he restored the old forge in the rear, hired an Iron Master, and began reproducing iron, partially to fill his own needs, and partially to satisfy a commercial need he felt existed in the marketplace.

Edward Guy was the Iron Master who worked for Nutting at the Saugus Iron Works from 1916-1921. Production increased fairly rapidly, with Nutting issuing a Sales Catalog in 1919, similar to his 1918 Windsor Chair Catalog. This Catalog, **Early American Ironwork**, was copyrighted 1919 by Wallace Nutting Inc. and included a wide variety of iron products that Nutting was commercially reproducing.

The Catalog was only 24 pages, much smaller than his Windsor Chair Catalog, but this **Early American Ironwork** Catalog displayed a much wider array of Iron products than most people would have realized. This Catalog included sections on Fireplace Furniture, Candlestands, Wall Sconces, Table Lights, Movable Candlesticks, Chandeliers, Door Knockers, Door Latches, Hinges, and even Weather Vanes.

Each particular piece of iron had a unique catalog number, just as his hand-colored pictures and reproduction furniture had specific catalog numbers. All iron products began with the capital letter 'I', followed by a 3-digit number.

Edward Guy, with Nutting's guidance, produced what were expected to be the best selling items in advance, stockpiling them for inventory. Those that could not be stockpiled would be made to order. Nutting claimed he was able to furnish the entire

Ironwork of the Pilgrim Century Made in 1918
A STATEMENT BY EDWARD GUY, MAKER OF HAND WROUGHT IRON

To Whom It May Concern: -

A copy of the book written by Wallace Nutting showing furniture and ironwork of the Pilgrim century was sent to me, and I thought it was strange business when I saw pictures of ironwork made by me a few years ago, now known as antique ironwork, for students and collectors to study.

I thought it was strange again when the last lines of the author are: "Finally the author begs a kindly judgment on his work, trusting it will be understood all has been guided by fidelity in dealing with the faithful artificers of the Pilgrim century."

For five years I made wrought iron for Wallace Nutting, Inc. Mr. Nutting wrote about my work and praised it. In a booklet given to the public in November, 1917, he wrote: "In Mr. Edward Guy, the mastersmith, he (Mr. Nutting) has secured a man who is a descendant of a line of forgemen of five generations. His ancestors were trained in the Lancashire region of England, famous for its cunning and beautiful wrought ironwork. The workmanship challenges comparison with anything of the sort produced in modern times. The daintiness of the work, together with it's feeling of taste, will certainly commend itself to all discriminating persons."

On page 559 of the Nutting book are two iron candleholders. Both were made by me in 1918. I have the original sketch used by me to make them, which was copied from a book called "Village Homes of England", page 157. They are from Sussex. We changed the candle sockets.

On page 553 of the Nutting book there is shown a pair of pipe tongs or brand tongs. They came out of the same book of English work. They are four years old. They are numbered 184. I also made 181 and 183, but they are copies of the old American tongs. I still have the shop drawings used to make the pair captured at some fort according to Nutting.

On page 573 there are nine door-knockers shown. I made every one of them, and seven out of the nine are my original designs. I have witnesses who saw me make them, and they will say so any time, anywhere.

All the illustrations in the Nutting book, with numbers on the pictures of ironwork, were taken from the catalogue of ironwork sold by Wallace Nutting, Inc. Why show catalogue numbers in a $15 book?

I have counted over 150 pieces shown in both the catalogue and the book. Old and new are mixed together. I make this statement in self defense, because I made much of the ironwork to be sold as modern in the old style, and I still make it.

Honest ironwork is my living. I want to keep the record straight.

Very truly yours,
Saugus Center, Mass., April 1, 1922   (Signed) EDWARD GUY

Text of Edward Guy Letter, dated April 1, 1922

hardware for any 17th or 18th century house, either from designs submitted by the purchaser or from his own personal designs.

The question of whether Nutting ever "invented" any "original" iron designs came into question several years after he opened the ironworks. In 1922, the year after Nutting released **Furniture of the Pilgrim Century,** and one year after he had left Nutting's employment, Edward Guy released a letter to bookstores and librarians who may have purchased **Furniture of the Pilgrim Century,** claiming that some of the iron that Nutting listed as original, was actually produced by Guy himself in 1918.

The reason Nutting would have tried to pass off his reproduction iron work as original is unclear, having never seen his response to the charges. I have a hard time believing that he would ever intentionally put himself into such an awkward position. Putting both his sometimes overzealous personality and his religious background aside, it's hard to believe that such a nationally renowned expert would put his reputation into question in order to earn what would literally amount to only a few dollars selling his door knockers.

One Nutting researcher speculated that perhaps *"Nutting simply thought there should have been seventeenth century American door knockers of the style designed and produced under his supervision."*

Or, perhaps several photographs were inadvertently switched and never caught until after the book's publication. After all, **Furniture of the Pilgrim Century** contained over 1000 photographs and the possibility exists that an honest mistake was made.

It is also unclear what caused Edward Guy to publicly humiliate Wallace Nutting. Whether there was bad blood after Guy left Nutting's employment in 1921, or whether Nutting himself simply refused to publicly acknowledge the mistake is unclear.

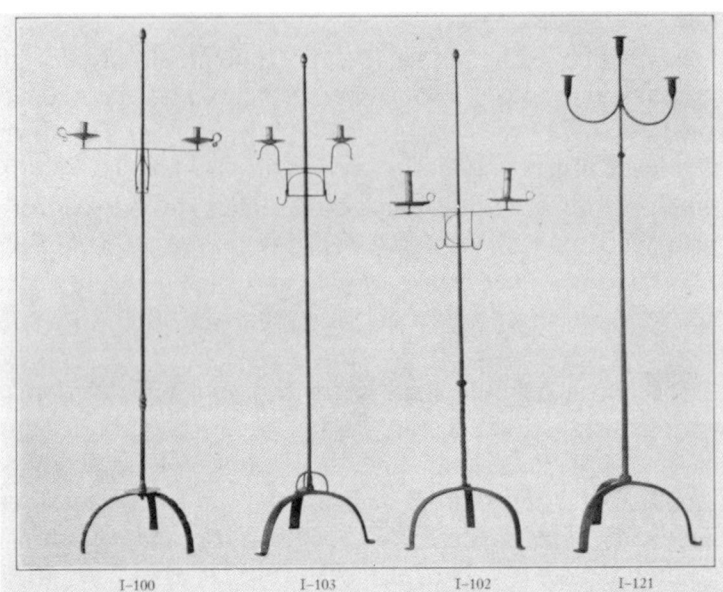

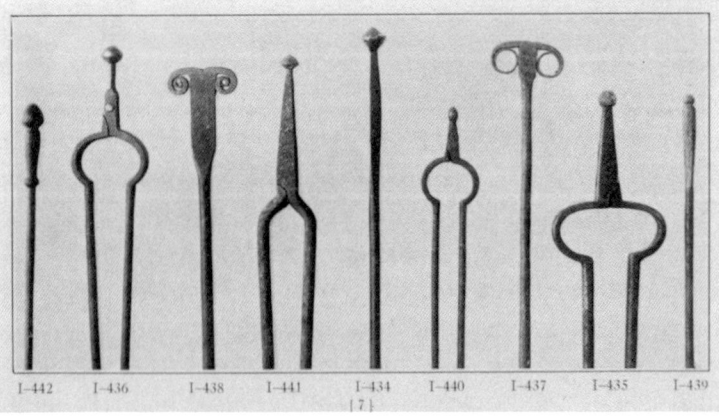

A page from **Early American Ironwork**

In any event, it would appear that Nutting's ironwork business never flourished the way he had hoped. Although it closed upon the sale of the Saugus Iron Works, he continued to offer his reproduction iron in the 1927, 1927-28, and 1930 Furniture Catalogs.

The biggest problem facing collectors today is that **none of Nutting's ironwork was marked.** Unlike his hand-colored pictures which carried the famous Wallace Nutting signature, or the reproduction furniture which contained either a Paper Label or Branded Signature, his iron was nearly impossible to mark.

And because Nutting never intended to mark his ironwork, positive identification is extremely difficult today. Because iron oxidizes and rusts so quickly, and now that his iron has had more than 70 years to age, separating Nutting's iron from the original is nearly impossible.

In the absence of any written documentation (e.g., sales receipts), pretty much the only way to positively identify a piece of Wallace Nutting iron is through a visual match with the item pictured in one of Nutting's sales catalogs.

Without a doubt nearly all Wallace Nutting reproduction ironwork is being sold as original today. Since it is always unmarked, it looks like original, and is sold as such...at original-iron prices. And since it is always unmarked, you will most likely have a difficult time convincing a dealer that his 'original' iron is actually a piece of unmarked Nutting iron. Therefore, expect to pay top dollar for it.

No production records are known to have been kept so there is no way of knowing exactly how much Wallace Nutting iron was sold.

Based on the limited amount I have seen, I would have to believe that relatively little was ever produced.

> **Rule of Thumb: Wallace Nutting iron was never signed. The only way to identify Nutting ironwork is through visual identification through one of his Catalogs.**

IRON PRICE LIST

Number	Latches	Price	Number		Price
I-1	Triangle latch, large	$10.00	I-31A	Butterfly, small	$4.50
I-1A	Triangle latch, small	7.00	I-32	Scrolled H large	5.50
I-2	Tulip bud, large	15.00	I-32A	Scrolled H small	4.50
I-2A	Tulip bud, small	11.00	I-33	Plain H large	3.50
I-3	Crescent and ball	15.00	I-33A	Plain H small	3.00
I-4	Open heart latch	22.00	I-34	Plain HL large	6.00
I-5	Flat ball and spear	16.00	I-34A	Plain HL small	5.00
I-6	Heart and point latch	12.00	I-35	Butterfly and strap	8.00
I-7	Pointed heart latch, large	12.00	I-36	Hammered HL small	5.00
I-7A	Pointed heart, small	8.00	I-38	Coxcomb, $3\frac{1}{2}$ x $8\frac{1}{4}$"	12.00
I-8	Hampden latch	24.00	I-39	Scrolled T, 6 x 9"	6.00
I-9	Ball and spear latch	17.00	I-119	Moravian scroll	$15 to 25.00
I-10	Combination knockers	20.00	I-127	Chest pins, pair	.50
I-10A	Knocker only	16.00	I-128	Strap chest hinge	4.00
I-11	Oval, large	7.00		Shutter Fasteners	
I-11A	Oval, small	6.00	I-80	Pair, outside	$2.50
	Hinges		I-81	Pair, outside	3.00
I-25	Serpentine L, 37"	$17.00	I-82	Pair, outside	2.50
I-26	Hammered HL hinge, large	12.00	I-83	Pair, outside	2.50
I-27	Tulip bud and blossom	35.00	I-51	Scrolled fastener	3.00
I-28	Pointed heart 31"	8.00	I-52	Fastener, inside	2.00
I-29	Pointed heart 24"	7.00	I-144	H door fastener	4.50
I-30	Archaic butterfly, large	4.00		Lighting Fixtures	
I-30A	Archaic butterfly, small	4.50	I-61	Floor stand, 3 light	$15.00
I-31	Butterfly, large	5.00	I-62	Floor stand, 2 light	18.00

[6]

Partial Wallace Nutting Ironwork Price List (1926)

IRON PRICE LIST — Concluded

Number		Price
I-63	Fine iron and brass, floor	$26.00
I-70	Adjustable, floor	20.00
I-71	Chandelier, wood hub, 6 light	30.00
I-72	Chandelier, all tin, 4 light	15.00
I-220	Tin candle sconce, sunburst	5.00
I-221	Tin candle sconce, narrow	2.00
I-222	Tin candle sconce, narrow, hand painted	4.00
I-232	Corner sconce, plain	6.00
I-233	Corner sconce, decorated	8.00
I-235	Oval, decorated, sconce	4.00
I-236	Oval with mirror, sconce	6.00
I-237	Single branch, sconce	9.00
I-238	Double branch, sconce	12.00

Fireplace Furniture

Number		Price
I-249	Cone head andirons	$16.00
I-250	Heart-shaped andirons	18.00
I-251	Goose head andirons	18.00
I-252	Octagon ball andirons	16.00
I-253	Spit hook attachment	2.00
I-254	Spit rod, pierced arrow point	4.00
I-255	Scroll head andirons	16.00
I-256	Small shoe base andirons	13.00
I-257	Brass tip andirons	20.00
I-258	Simple crane	5.00
I-259	Scrolled small crane	7.00
I-260	Scrolled large crane	10.00
I-261	Crane eyes	1.00
I-264	Pot hooks, large simple	.50
I-265	Pot hooks, twisted	1.00
I-266	Long shovels, simple	5.00
I-267	Wrought scrolled poker	2.50
I-277	Trivet, simple, small	4.00
I-278	Trivet, simple, large	7.00
I-279	Trivet, scrolled	10.00
I-280	Trivet, elaborate	16.00
I-281	Skewer holder, simple	4.00
I-282	Skewer holder, scrolled	6.00
I-283	Skewer holder, heart motive	7.00
I-284	Skewers, each	.35
I-448	Jamb hooks, twisted	4.00
I-449	Jamb hooks	4.50

Bolts, Etc.

Number		Price
I-270	Heavy door bolts, top, each	$10.00
I-271	Heavy door bolts, bottom, each	6.00
I-272	Square bolts, 4" plain	3.00
I-273	Square bolts, 4" scrolled	4.00
I-274	Square bolts, 8" plain	4.50
I-275	Square bolts, 8" scrolled	$5.50
I-450	Wrought nails, small, 100	2.50
I-451	Wrought nails, large, 100	3.00
I-452	Rag nails, 3", each	.10

Furniture Brasses
Mostly made for us, by hand

Sizes measured from center to center of post holes.

Number		Price
B-1	Oval pulls "Eagle," 3 x 2⅜", each	$0.75
B-6	Oval pulls, oak branch, 4 x 2"	.65
B-N7	Oval escutcheons	.25
B-8	Oval pulls, scrolled, 3¼ x 2⅛"	.75
B-9	Pulls, 2½"	1.20
	Escutcheon to match	.90
B-23	Pulls, 2½"	.85
	Escutcheons to match	.55
B-25	Pulls, 2¾"	1.25
	Escutcheons to match	.95
	Pulls, 3½"	1.55
	Escutcheons to match	1.25
	Pulls, 3¾"	1.70
	Escutcheons to match	1.40
B-35	Plain round or oval Sheraton pulls, 3¼"	.95
	Plain round or Sheraton pulls, 3½"	1.05
B-50	Pulls, 2¼"	1.65
	Escutcheons to match	1.35
B-51	Pulls, 2½"	1.80
	Escutcheons to match	1.55
B-N52	Pulls with 1¾" drop	1.20
B-53	Escutcheons, 2¼"	1.35
B-54	Pulls, 2"	1.85
	Escutcheons to match	1.65
B-70	Escutcheons 4" long	.75
B-N80	Tear drop pulls, 1¾"	.90
B-N81	Escutcheons to match	.25
B-N82	Small pull, ½", $0.18; ¾"	.22
B-N83	Large pulls, 1", $0.25; 1¼"	.30
B-N84	Knobs, ¼"	.15
B-N85	" ½"	.18
B-N86	" ⅝"	.20
B-N87	" ¾"	.25
B-88	Ring pulls	1.20
B-N89	Small knobs	1.00
B-N90	Bed post cover	.45
B-N91	Bed post cover	.40
B-N92	Small ring pull, 2"	.40
B-N93	Escutcheons to match	.32
B-N94	Large knobs	1.05

Partial Wallace Nutting Ironwork Price List (1926)

A Transition Double Comb Back Windsor
with Script Branded Signature...Sold at Auction for $1100.00

Chapter 6

The Transition Years...1922-23

Nutting sold only Windsors for the first several years. Beginning with only a few different Windsor forms in 1917, he expanded his product line so quickly that by 1918 his Windsor Chair Catalog included over 100 different variations of chairs, beds, stools, cradles, cribs, bassinets, love seats, and settees, all using the Windsor design.

By 1920, Nutting began to study and copy other forms of antique furniture: chests, tables, desks, and cabinet pieces. Although his production of non-Windsor chair pieces at this time wasn't very large, he did find himself having some initial success in his new endeavors.

Business was growing so well that Nutting decided to consolidate both the picture and furniture business in Ashland, Massachusetts. In 1920 he purchased an old canning factory which was especially attractive because it had its own railway spur enabling Nutting to receive raw materials and ship finished goods by rail. Apparently Nutting borrowed a considerable sum of money to complete this move because he later stated that he owed $120,000 due to his enlarged studio and facility.

The business still continued to use Paper Labels for identification at Ashland, although modified somewhat from earlier labels.

But at the same time, Nutting found himself beginning to think of retirement again. His first retirement was short-lived. As a matter of fact, it was almost no retirement at all. In 1904 he seemed to jump from the ministry directly into his first picture studio in New York City, and then into his new Southbury studio in 1905 where business interests began to take over his life.

His seemingly immediate career change from the ministry into a successful, profit-making business caused some people to accuse him, albeit under their breath, of leaving the cloth in order to make money. Although he continued to deny it to his dying days, some people just never understood how he could leave the ministry because of its hectic pace, only to enter a profession that kept him even busier.

Regardless of the circumstances surrounding his first retirement, after more than fifteen years in the picture business Nutting once again began to consider retirement. With his picture business booming...with his Windsor chair business growing...with several books already successfully published...and with a name that was nationally known and respected...Nutting decided to sell all business interests. This time, he intended to *enjoy* his retirement and pursue a less-exhausting career... collecting and studying early American antiques.

So in 1922, eighteen years after his first retirement, Wallace Nutting sold all business interests and retired...for a second time. He sold his entire picture business and his furniture business, **along with the right to continue using the Wallace Nutting name.** It appears that he received somewhere around $100,000 from the sale of the business itself, and additional money from the sale of the real estate.

Nutting used the proceeds to pay off creditors for debts arising from his Ashland expansion and to begin what we have already described as **Phase II** of his antique collecting career.

Nutting began his retirement enjoyably enough, studying antiques wherever he could locate them. He attended auctions, traveled to near and distant antique shops, toured museums, and visited dealers and friends, buying new pieces when he could, studying, recording, and photographing when he could not buy. Within the next year his keen eye, high energy level, and new-found bankroll enabled him to begin to accumulate what was soon to become one of the finest antique collections ever assembled...all within one year of his latest 'retirement'.

But by 1923, things began to trouble him. Undoubtedly retirement didn't suit him. He didn't sit still very long after his first retirement so there was no reason to believe he would relax after his second retirement either.

But what disturbed him the most was what he observed happening to the business still bearing his name. Although whatever contractual agreements had been reached between Nutting and the new owners are unclear, there's no doubt that Nutting expected them to continue with the same high level of quality that had been associated with the Wallace Nutting name over the past eighteen years.

They did not.

Records are not clear as to whom Nutting sold the business. According to a former colorist, it was a "Chair Company in Fitchburg". Regardless of the new owner's name, Nutting was **outraged** at the poor quality of the products being produced and sold by this company...**still using the Wallace Nutting name.** How **dare they** cheapen the good name that he had worked so long and hard to achieve!

The quality of the Wallace Nutting hand-colored pictures deteriorated horribly. Although they were still using Nutting's original model pictures and negatives, the coloring was awful. Colors were not nearly as bright or cheerful as before, and the detail began to look muddy and murky... more like a bad water color than a hand-tinted platinotype picture. One colorist complained that the new owners were more interested in quantity than quality.

* * * * *

The quality of Wallace Nutting furniture deteriorated as well. Although they were following Wallace Nutting's patterns and models, they began to cut corners in order to reduce costs...something that Nutting would **never** approve of.

The newer Nutting furniture...marked by a distinctive **Script Branded Signature**...were no longer exact copies of the earlier reproductions (See page 102 for a sample of the Script Signature). At first glance, these newer reproductions looked good, and were probably better than most other reproductions of the period. But upon a closer look, the quality just wasn't the same as when Nutting himself controlled the process.

The differences between this transition furniture and Nutting-produced furniture were obvious. For example, when Nutting owned the company, the Windsor seats were all carved from one **solid 2" plank**; the transition seats were carved from a piece of wood consisting of five smaller pieces of wood glued together. Under the new owners, height specifications were not always followed, the shaping of seats were not nearly as detailed or pronounced, and carvings on the ears were not always as sharp and crisp as before.

On tables, narrower boards were used; on dressers and case pieces, drawers were frequently constructed without dovetailing; and on desks and cabinet pieces, the carvings were either omitted or greatly simplified.

Less expensive woods were frequently used. For example, Welsh Cupboards were made from cheaper maple instead of the more expensive oak. More often than not, the standard finish became the darker mahogany style, regardless of whether the original specifications called for it. And fewer coats of finish were applied.

Anyway, these deviations from the old Nutting way of doing things may not have been visible to most people, but they were certainly noticeable to him. By 1923, he decided to end his second retirement and buy his company back.

He did have one major problem, however...**money**. He had used the proceeds he had originally obtained in 1922 to pay off his creditors and to purchase antiques. But he did have one ready source of funds...**his own personal antique collection**.

Although Nutting may not have been a rich individual, neither was he poor. His national reputation as author, businessman, and authority on antiques had put him in touch with many wealthy collectors...Ford...DuPont...Garvan...Sack...Erving...and J.P. Morgan. (the same J.P.Morgan whose grandfather formerly lived in the Cutler-Bartlet House, one of the homes in Nutting's Colonial Chain).

Anyway, Nutting negotiated the sale of his personal antique collection to J.P. Morgan for approximately $90,000, who in turn, donated it to the Wadsworth Atheneum in Hartford, Connecticut.

Nutting immediately used that money to repurchase his picture and furniture business and set out to restore his good name.

* * * * *

The question arises whether furniture with the **Script Branded Signature** is indeed "Wallace Nutting Furniture". I've always maintained that although the quality of the 'Script' furniture is not as good as the Paper Label or Block Branded pieces, it's still better than most other 20th century reproductions. It was made from the

Transition Period Seats Were Constructed of 5 Glued Pieces

original Nutting patterns and designs, it followed Nutting's original numbering identification system, was sold under the Wallace Nutting name, and therefore should be considered Wallace Nutting furniture. However, because of its somewhat lower quality, value should be adjusted downward.

How much furniture with the Script Signature was produced? No one knows because no production records from the transition years are known to exist. But there does seem to have been quite a bit produced. Based on the large quantity of Nutting furniture I have seen, I would estimate that perhaps 15% of Nutting furniture has a Script Signature.

Let's put this into perspective. Nutting was producing furniture for approximately twenty years, with the greatest volume in the mid-1920's. The 1922-1923 production period translates roughly into 8% of total production (1.5 years out of 20). Yet, I have estimated that 15% of the furniture has the Script Signature.

How could a company just starting in the business have produced such a large amount of furniture in such a short time? The most logical answer is that since they had purchased Nutting's furniture designs, patterns, models, and equipment, their start-up time was minimal. And, because they cut so many corners, they were able to produce more furniture per day than when Nutting himself ran the company.

Did Nutting himself ever **produce** furniture with the Script Branded Signature? Although there has been some speculation that Nutting may have first started using the Script Signature himself just prior to selling his business in 1922, I have been unable to find any confirming evidence to support this. I have seen a few Wallace Nutting **furniture advertisements**, with the Ashland address, that contained a Script Signature in the advertising copy, but I haven't been able to confirm through any other source whether Nutting did indeed use the Script Branded Signature himself.

In the absence of any confirming evidence that Nutting had used the Script Signature, you will be safe with the following guideline:

> **Rule of Thumb: Furniture with the Script Branded Signature was produced between 1922-23, and was made when Nutting did not own the Company.**

Did Nutting himself ever **sell** furniture with the detested Script Signature? Somewhat surprisingly, yes.

Several years ago I purchased an entire dining room set, including a gate-leg table and four Windsor chairs, all with the Script Signature. Accompanying the furniture was a letter indicating that the owner had purchased the set **directly from Wallace Nutting himself** while in Framingham in 1936. My speculation is that when Nutting repurchased the business in 1923, he must have also purchased any existing inventory bearing the Script Branded Signature. Rather than destroy it, he most likely stockpiled it and sold it at reduced prices, especially when business deteriorated during the 1930's.

Anyway, you should be aware that any Wallace Nutting furniture bearing the Script Signature was manufactured during 1922-23 and was of an inferior quality when compared to furniture produced when Nutting himself owned the company.

> **Rule of Thumb: Furniture bearing the Script Branded Signature may be worth anywhere from 25%-50% less than an identical piece bearing a Paper Label or Block Branded Signature.**

With things firmly back in his control in 1923, after his second unsuccessful retirement, Nutting was now ready to begin some of his grandest accomplishments of all.

Chapter 7

Other Wallace Nutting Furniture

By the time Nutting had resumed control of his business, he had already accomplished more than most individuals could hope to accomplish in a lifetime:

> * His picture business had been grossing upwards of $1000 per day, making him undoubtedly the most successful marketer of hand-colored photographs of his era
> * He was already a recognized expert in the field of antiques, writing technical articles for many magazines and newspapers, and being sought out by the top furniture collectors and scholars of his day
> * He had successfully published **American Windsors**, the first definitive book ever published on Windsor Chairs
> * His furniture company was producing Windsor furniture that was unsurpassed in quality anywhere
> * He had purchased and restored five historic New England homes, opening them to help educate the general public on how our ancestors lived
> * He had operated an Iron Works business that made some of the finest early iron ever reproduced
> * He had just published **Furniture of the Pilgrim Century**, the boldest attempt yet by anyone attempting to historically document early American furniture

But **Furniture of the Pilgrim Century**, published in 1921, only seemed to whet his appetite for new challenges. Just as he learned how to reproduce Windsor chairs after his extensive study of the Windsor form, Nutting now found himself desiring to reproduce other forms of early furniture as well.

A Three-Back Pilgrim Chair...Block Brand...#493
Described by Nutting as "The Most Massive And Most Comfortable of All Early Chairs

So upon resuming control of his furniture business, Nutting began to expand his furniture reproduction operation beyond Windsor chairs. One of his earliest catalogs issued upon his resuming control is only 32 pages, picturing approximately 70 of the nearly 250 designs he was reproducing at that time. In addition to his wide selection of 18th century Windsor chair designs, Nutting was producing 17th century oak and maple cabinet and turned pieces, along with a select few 18th century pine and maple cupboards, chairs, chests, tables, and desks. Only a few pieces were available in walnut.

At this point Nutting had little interest in the later Queen Anne, Chippendale, Hepplewhite, and Sheraton styles. His primary interests were in the late 17th and early 18th century furniture that he photographed for his **Furniture of the Pilgrim Century** book. His catalog stated that he was capable of copying any article of furniture known to have been used before 1720, and he carried his pine and maple reproductions up through 1780. He used very little mahogany and stopped just short of the cabriole leg.

Some of his earlier reproduction pieces included court cupboards; paneled and sunflower chests; oak chest of drawers; butterfly, gateleg, refractory, trestle, folding gate, and tavern tables; framed desks; ladderback chairs; joined and rushed stools; pilgrim and carver chairs; and even a day bed and bible box.

By the mid 1920's, furniture sales were increasing. The country's economy was fairly stable, and America had a renewed interest in early American furniture. Although furniture sales were not yet profitable, they were encouraging. And with his picture business thriving, Nutting expected that the picture business would be able to carry the furniture business until it began to generate a profit.

One Drawer Oak Chest, with Black Ornaments...Block Brand...#909
(Gordon Gray Collection)

Pine Trestle Table...Block Brand...#615

At his peak, Nutting employed a group of approximately twenty-five craftsmen whom he described in one of his Furniture Catalogs as *"fine American mechanics, men of character, whom it is a privilege to know. Many live on their own little farms. They are trained experts in their lines - turners, chair, and cabinet makers. My greatest asset is these men sought out from every direction, men who love their work, and who are cooperating with me to produce the finest forms of furniture"*. (In reality, many of the furniture makers he employed were foreign born. Nutting seem to feel that foreign-born craftsmen possessed finer skills and were better disciplined than their American counterparts.)

By 1927-1928, economic reality began to set it. Sales had not picked up to where he would have liked and expenses were running higher than anticipated. Whereas his earlier Furniture Catalog stated that he stopped short of the cabriole leg and pieces made of mahogany, by 1927 he found it necessary to copy some of those later Queen Anne, Chippendale, Hepplewhite, and Sheraton styles that he had condemned only a few years earlier. Perhaps he didn't like these higher styles as much as the earlier 17th century oak and maple styles...but the public did. If he wished to remain in business, he would have to adapt to the public's taste.

Expanding beyond Windsor chairs and the Pilgrim and William & Mary styles, this catalog included Savery Highboys and Lowboys, Queen Anne, Chippendale, and Hepplewhite arm and side chairs, carved walnut sideboards, a Goddard chest-on-chest, Pine and Welsh dressers, and a carved corner cupboard. In all, Nutting was offering 80 different types of chairs, 30 beds, 60 tables, 20 chests and chest of drawers, 20 cupboards, and 20 desks and secretaries.

Also by the 1927-28, not only had Nutting yielded to the later styles of furniture, he began commercially adapting his antique designs to items which had no true antique precedent. His stated

Spoon Rack, Carved, in Original Red Paint...#903
This piece had no markings and was verified through a Furniture Catalog.

purpose for these adaptations was strictly to satisfy a legitimate market demand but, in reality, this was an attempt to bolster sagging furniture sales. He created a commercial line of furniture which adapted his furniture to a business setting: bank check writing desks, typewriter desks, executive desks, stenographer's chairs, spinning wheel hat racks, and even an oak radiator cover.

It is also interesting to note that by this time, Nutting had expanded the scope of his business operations considerably to include such diverse services as:

* Furniture reproduction
* Hook rugs
* Hardware consisting of hinges, latches, window fastenings, fireplace utinsels, sconces, and lighting fixtures
* Panels, mantels, and door heads
* Simple and elaborate carvings
* Hand-colored pictures of all types
* Small calendars
* Illustrations of estates, the interleaving of illustrations, enlargements, and coloring on order (e.g., **Up at the Vilas Farm**)
* Consultation with home owners and architects regarding the architectural aspects of homes
* Interior decorating consultation for homes
* Interior decorating consultation for banks, clubs, hospitals, and offices
* Antique repair and restoration
* A series of lectures on furniture, colonial interiors, and architecture, offering three thousand subjects

Here was a man who only a few short years ago had "retired". Now, by 1927, he expanded his business operations to include an incredibly wide variety of services.

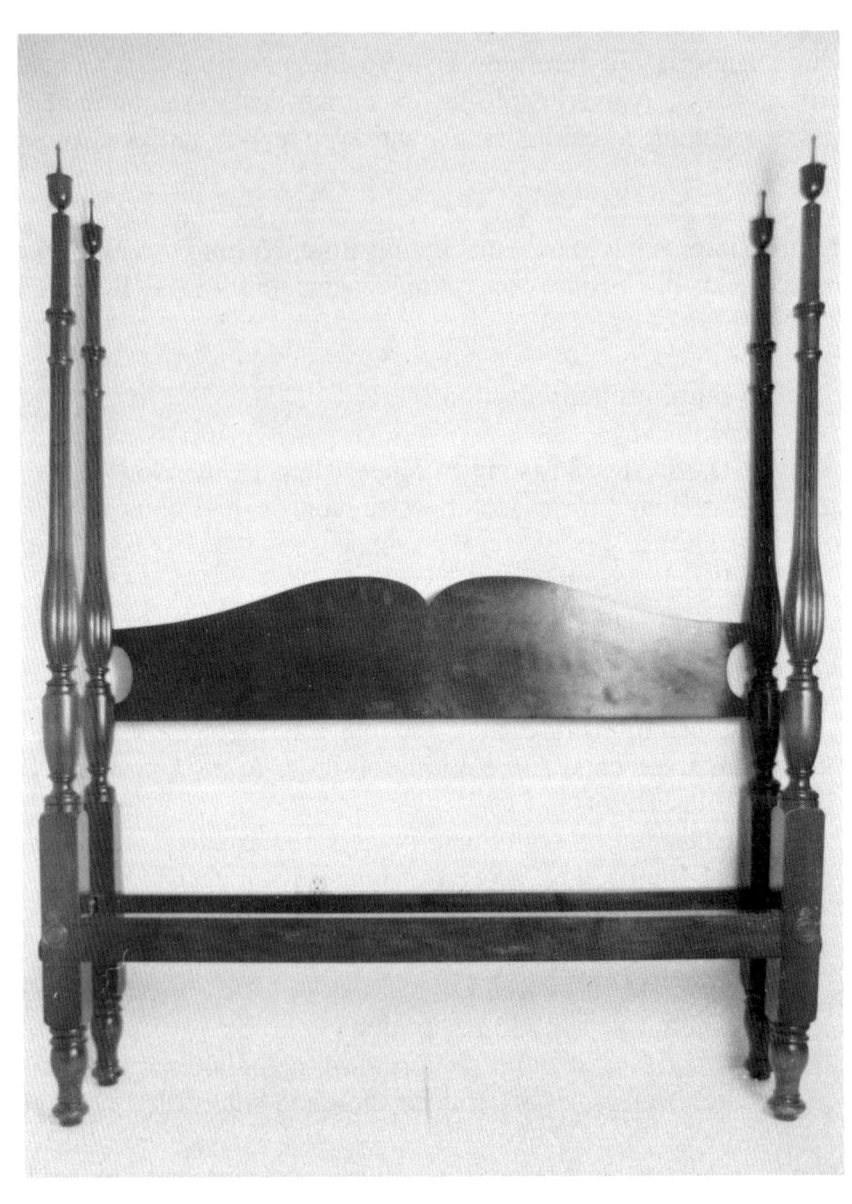

Mahogany, Reeded Sheraton Bed...Block Brand...#846B

* * * * *

One of his customers eventually became Colonial Williamsburg. After unsuccessfully searching for authentic period furniture to use in one of their restored buildings, they commissioned Nutting to produce a set of twelve Flemish arm chairs in 1932. In a move that was characteristically Nutting, he produced the entire set of twelve chairs the way **he** felt they should have been made prior to receiving approval from the Williamsburg Trustees on the initial model.

Quite unexpectedly, the entire set was rejected as unacceptable. Whether the error was the result of Nutting's personal interpretation of the chairs, whether his craftsmen were unable to read his cryptic style of writing, or whether Williamsburg simply failed to provide clear enough direction really doesn't matter. After considerable debate regarding the merits of his chairs, Nutting produced twelve chairs that were acceptable to Williamsburg and was paid $112.50 each. He then resold the twelve 'incorrect' chairs privately.

Regardless of the unusual circumstances surrounding these twelve chairs, the fact that such a prestigious foundation as Colonial Williamsburg selected Nutting above all other furniture makers in the country exemplifies the high degree of acceptance and respect there was for Wallace Nutting's furniture. These chairs are still on display today in the Colonial Williamsburg Council Chambers.

* * * * *

The construction methods and techniques outlined in the chapter on Windsor chairs were similar in scope to the techniques followed on his other furniture. Nutting would first identify the piece of furniture he wished to copy. He would then study and analyze it, create scaled drawings, make whatever "improvements" he felt

Maple, New England Five-Back Ladderback Arm Chair
Block Brand...#490

were necessary, produce the Model components, and then begin production.

The sources for Nutting's reproductions came from many places. Some were antiques that Nutting had privately purchased, generally with the intention of copying. Or sometimes he would borrow the original from a friend or acquaintance. And sometimes he would base his reproduction upon an original antique found in a Museum, frequently either the Metropolitan Museum in New York City or the Wadsworth Atheneum which housed his former collection.

You should understand that Nutting was not a craftsman himself. He never lifted a tool, nor did he have any mechanical ability. His major asset was his keen eye for beauty. Nutting knew better than most how to identify a beautiful piece of furniture, but he relied upon his craftsmen to actually reproduce it for him.

It should also be understood that Nutting didn't accomplish everything at once. Each step in his career was a growing process, and each success led to new confidence in his next undertaking. His successful reproduction of his first Windsor chair led to his copying of more than 100 different Windsor designs. His success with Windsor chairs led to his copying non-Windsor chairs; his success with non-Windsor chairs led to copying tables; tables led to chests; and chests led to larger cabinet pieces.

Nutting claimed his biggest challenge was his reproduction of a Goddard blockfront secretary with nine shell carvings. This was one of his earliest attempts at copying a mahogany piece and he knew that if he could successfully copy this secretary, he could reproduce anything.

He took six of his workmen to Providence, Rhode Island to analyze

Pine, Wing Back Settle...Block Brand...#416

the piece. They studied it, took measurements, made sketches, and photographed it. When final work was completed, Nutting was pleased with what he considered to be his finest reproduction ever. Only six were produced, **with a 1927 retail price of $1450.**

As with his Windsor chairs, his non-Windsor furniture was manufactured in the best manner possible, using the finest woods available. Each worker was obligated to follow the original Model *exactly*. To insure adherence to his high level of quality, Nutting posted his "10 Furniture Construction Commandments" above each craftsmen's work bench:

Wallace Nutting Furniture Construction
Ten Construction Commandments

1. All work to be of the best quality.
2. If the old method is the best, use it.
3. If the work can be done better by hand, do it that way.
4. Use long and large mortises, and large square white oak pins.
5. Make all joined work fit together perfectly, using draw bore where it is better.
6. Match the color where two pieces come together.
7. Follow the sample strictly. Take no liberties.
8. The hand and the mouth do not work effectively at the same time.
9. Keep busy, do your best, and no fault will be found.
10. Let nothing leave your hands until you are proud of the work.

To Insure Individuality and Make Men While Making Furniture.

Spinning Wheel Hat Rack...Block Brand...#40

Treen Salt Dish...Punched Name...#35

At his peak, Wallace Nutting had produced an incredibly wide variety of furniture styles and designs:

* Periods ranged from early Pilgrim and William & Mary, through and including Queen Anne, Chippendale, Hepplewhite, and Sheraton

* Dates ranged from 1620-1830

* Specific designs included arm chairs, beds, chests, clocks, corner cupboards, court cupboards, desks, dressers, high boys, low boys, mirrors, settees, settles, side chairs, sofas, tables, treen ware...and more than 100 variations of the Windsor chair

Wallace Nutting had copied more than 500 different forms of early American antiques...more than anyone else before him...or since. His reproductions were among the 20th century's best. The quality was excellent and the designs were diverse enough to furnish any style of home. But there was one important ingredient missing from Wallace Nutting's furniture business.

He was never able to turn a profit.

Wallace Nutting - 1938

Chapter 8

The Decline of the Wallace Nutting Furniture Company

Even with the release of his 1927-28 Furniture Catalog, and despite his ever expanding line of reproduction styles, Nutting was still operating the furniture business at a loss. Lower-than-anticipated sales obviously contributed to this lack of profit.

Also contributing to the furniture company's losses were the unexpectedly high production costs he incurred. The high expenses certainly didn't come from high salaries, as Nutting was not known to have been overly generous with his employees.

Rather, the high expenses came from the inordinate amount of time spent producing each piece. As explained in the chapter on Windsor chairs, and as dictated in his "10 Commandments", Nutting stubbornly adhered to his desire to do things by the old method. No corners were cut, regardless of cost, in order to produce a piece of furniture worthy of the Wallace Nutting name. Wood workers were shaping only three Windsor seats per day, while refinishers could only turn out three chairs...on a good day.

And to further complicate matters, Nutting would frequently change his mind about furniture designs and specifications.

Nutting would all too frequently approve a Model and then, after actual production began, would make several changes. These changes wouldn't significantly alter the appearance of a piece, but *would* necessitate significant additional work. Sometimes he would add 3/4" to a leg, other times he would slightly change the height of a chest. But his constant meddling would require creating new scaled drawings, cutting new patterns, and preparing new models, thereby adding to overall production costs significantly. But what was even worse, these changes would take several key employees away from the actual production of furniture, which is what really paid the bills.

It didn't really matter whether Nutting was right or not, he didn't care. It was **his** furniture, it carried **his** name, and he wanted it to be perfect. He wanted things done **his** way, regardless of cost.

He always believed that despite his early losses, eventually the furniture business would turn a profit. And even if it was having minor losses, the profits from the picture business would be able to carry it along.

But something quite unexpected occurred in 1929...the Stock Market crashed and the country fell into the Great Depression. The resulting economic chaos severely impacted both Nutting's picture and furniture businesses.

One important factor you must understand is that Wallace Nutting's picture market was entirely different than his furniture market. The purchasers of Wallace Nutting pictures were generally middle and lower-middle class households. Nutting's hand-colored pictures were quite inexpensive, and as a result, were widely purchased by those individuals who could not afford finer forms of art.

It was also these same middle and lower-middle class households that were the most severely impacted by the crash. With unemployment running around 30%, those families who lost their jobs obviously stopped buying Wallace Nutting pictures. Unfortunately for Nutting, those who still retained their jobs stopped buying his pictures as well. With the economy so uncertain, very few households were willing to spend their precious cash on something so unneccesary as a Wallace Nutting picture.

On the other hand, the purchasers of Nutting's furniture were generally **not** the same middle and lower-middle class households who purchased his pictures. The primary market for Wallace Nutting furniture was upper middle and upper class households. These individuals had a much greater overall appreciation for fine antiques, and consequently, for Nutting's furniture. They were generally less severely impacted by the economic uncertainties of the depression, and as a group had more disposable income.

The **Wallace Nutting General Catalog, Supreme Edition**, contains a Price List for Nutting's reproductions dated February 1, 1932...*in the heart of the Depression.* Here is a sampling of some prices:

* A set of four #343 Chippendale Side Chairs... **$1200.00**
* A #579 Sheraton Settee...**$495.00**
* A #682b carved Sheraton Sideboard...**$650.00**
* A #992 carved Savory Highboy...**$1230.00**
* And the same #773 Goddard Block Front Secretary with nine shell Carvings that cost $1450 in 1927...**$1800.00**

And this was when admission to a movie was only a nickel.

The point I am trying to impress upon you is that Wallace Nutting furniture was not inexpensive. At a time when many families were worrying where their next meal was coming from, Wallace Nutting was trying to market furniture that many families could not afford even today.

Not surprisingly, the furniture business continued to lose money during the 1930's. His high prices, resulting from his stubborn refusal to lower his quality standards, basically pre-determined that he would continue to operate at a loss.

But, with the decline in picture sales, the once-profitable picture business was no longer capable of subsidizing the never-profitable furniture business.

By the early 1930's, the fate of Wallace Nutting's furniture business was pretty much inevitable. If he was unable to make a profit selling his furniture when the economy was stable, it was quite unlikely that he would be able to turn things around in the midst of a major economic depression.

By the mid 1930's, sales were off in all areas of the business. In 1936 Nutting had estimated that the furniture business had already lost more than $100,000. Although he always felt that 'providence' would provide, it never did, and he was forced to begin laying off some of his employees.

At one point cash was so tight that he tried paying off his employees with unsold furniture. Some accepted the furniture in lieu of their weekly pay. Those who could not accept furniture received personal cash advances from Nutting's bookkeeper. (Nutting eventually repaid Donnelly for these loans).

Things reached the point where the furniture inventory was growing rather than shrinking. Rather than laying off his last few remaining trained craftsmen, Nutting kept them employed for as long as possible. He would sell one chair from inventory and then make five more to replace it. Even price reductions couldn't rejuvenate sales.

Nutting stayed active in the business right to his dying days. However, by the spring of 1941, his visits to the studio became less frequent and of shorter duration. Most of the day-to-day business activities were carried on by the shop foreman and Ernest Donnelly.

* * * * *

Wallace Nutting died on July 19, 1941 of chronic cardiac degeneration. He was laid to rest in the Mt. Pleasant Cemetary in Augusta, Maine.

Mrs. Nutting inherited the entire Wallace Nutting estate, including the picture and furniture businesses, Wallace Nutting's remaining collection of antiques...and more than $100,000 in debt. Apparently Mrs. Nutting was unaware of their mounting bills and the fact that the furniture business had always been a losing venture.

In order to raise needed capital, Mrs. Nutting was forced to sell Nutting's remaining collection of authentic American antiques at auction. The sale was conducted by Parke-Bernet (now Sotheby's) on October 4, 1941 at their New York Galleries. The 200 lots sold for slightly more than $20,000, which was considerably less than expected. Apparently the market was fairly soft at the time and several experts later indicated that had Mrs. Nutting been able to wait several more years before selling, she probably would have done much better.

With the continued assistance of long-term employees Ernest John Donnelly and Esther Svenson, Mrs. Nutting carried on all aspects of the business until her death in August, 1944, at the age of 90.

The picture business was left to Ernest Donnelly and Esther Svenson. They jointly continued selling pictures until 1946 when Ernest Donnelly sold his share of the business to Miss Svenson.

Donnelly eventually moved to Philadelphia where he worked as an antique dealer until moving back to Ireland in 1970, where he died in 1973.

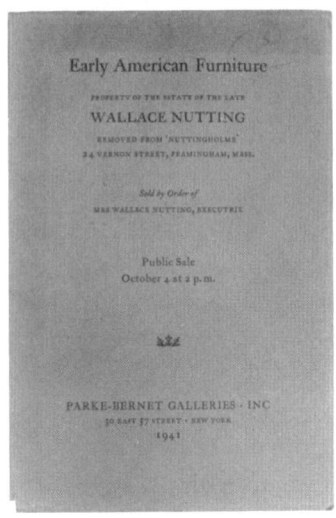

Parke-Bernet Catalog for Auction of Wallace Nutting's Estate

The Log House, Berea College, houses 3 rooms of Nutting furniture

Esther Svenson continued the picture business on a very limited basis, working out of her home. She died in 1972, leaving many Wallace Nutting momentos to the Framingham Public Library where many are displayed today. The remaining items were left to her sister, Hilda Cushing, who shared many items with Wallace Nutting collectors over the years.

Nutting's will also left a cash bequest of $1000 to his chauffer and gardener, John Kelly. Other gifts ranging from $500-$1000 were left to several nieces and nephews.

But having never had any children, and with no close relatives still living, Mrs. Nutting willed the remainder of her estate to Berea College, a long-term favorite charity of the Nuttings.

Berea College

Apparently Nutting's connection with the religiously oriented College began in the late 1890's when he first visited Kentucky. Nutting was impressed with the beauty surrounding Berea and was fascinated with the concept of a liberal arts school for Appalachian area students who could not afford college. In exchange for college tuition, students worked reproducing furniture which would be resold to help pay college expenses.

In 1900 Nutting delivered the commencement address at Berea. He continued to visit the college periodically in later years and formed a close friendship with several of the College's Presidents.

By the time he had started his furniture business, his association with Berea became even closer. On various occasions Nutting took several of his workmen to Berea to learn their secrets of making colonial furniture, and Nutting trained several Berea instructors at his furniture factory in Framingham.

During the 1930's, Nutting served as a Consultant to the College's Woodcraft Department, providing the college with many blueprinted furniture designs. Prior to Nutting's intervention, the students generally were selling only simple items such as stools and magazine racks. Nutting's designs enabled them to begin making more complex pieces such as welsh cupboards, corner cupboards, chairs, tables, and hanging cupboards.

Through their many years of association with the college, both Mr. and Mrs. Nutting had agreed that most of the furniture business should be left to Berea. Upon her death, Mrs. Nutting basically left everything in the estate to the college. Nuttingholme was sold by Berea to the First Parish Unitarian Universalist Church, which later demolished the home and turned the property into the church's parking lot.

All remaining, unsold Wallace Nutting reproduction furniture was transported to Berea for display and use around the college. In 1945, three shipments totaling 196 pieces of furniture arrived via B&A Railroad. Today, much of this Wallace Nutting furniture is on permanent display, occupying three rooms upstairs at **The Log House**, the retail outlet for the college's crafts industries.

Drexel Furniture Company

After all patterns and blueprints were copied for the college's use, Nutting's Framingham furniture factory, along with the rest of the furniture business, was sold to a furniture company in Drexel, North Carolina. This new company purchased the right to produce furniture with the Wallace Nutting name as part of Wallace Nutting Furniture, Inc., a Delaware Corporation, with its principal place of business at Framingham, Massachusetts.

Although it had been reported that Drexel never did anything with the Nutting furniture business because it proved to be too costly,

Drexel Heritage Furnishing Inc. (Drexel, NC) reported in 1983 that they had indeed made some earlier Nutting reproductions after purchasing manufacturer's rights shortly after Nutting's death. Files were no longer available regarding exactly what had been produced.

Drexel also produced several collections, or series of Nutting furniture in the 1950's. One collection, Drexel's **Wallace Nutting New Cherry Highlands "D" Collection**, was introduced in 1954 and discontinued in 1957.

Similar Drexel Wallace Nutting collections included: **"C" Nutting Maple** (January 1954-1957); **"F" Framingham Genuine Mahogany** (January 1954-1957); **607-657-687 American Treasury** (October 1960-1964); and **141-142-144-146 Wallace Nutting** (October 1960-1968).

Apparently very little of the Drexel furniture was ever produced. I have only seen a few pieces and the quality does not come close to resembling the earlier Nutting reproductions. Rather, the pieces I have seen look more like 1950's 'used' furniture than a 1920's bench made reproduction.

Drexel pieces seem to be branded with the name **Wallace Nutting, by Drexel.** This Nutting/Drexel furniture is not, and should not, be considered true Wallace Nutting furniture. Value should be determined by what it really is...1950's second-hand furniture, **not** legitimate Wallace Nutting reproductions. In my opinion, the name 'Wallace Nutting' adds nothing to the value of a piece of Drexel furniture.

And with the discontinuance of the last of the Drexel Collections, so ends the story of Wallace Nutting reproduction furniture.

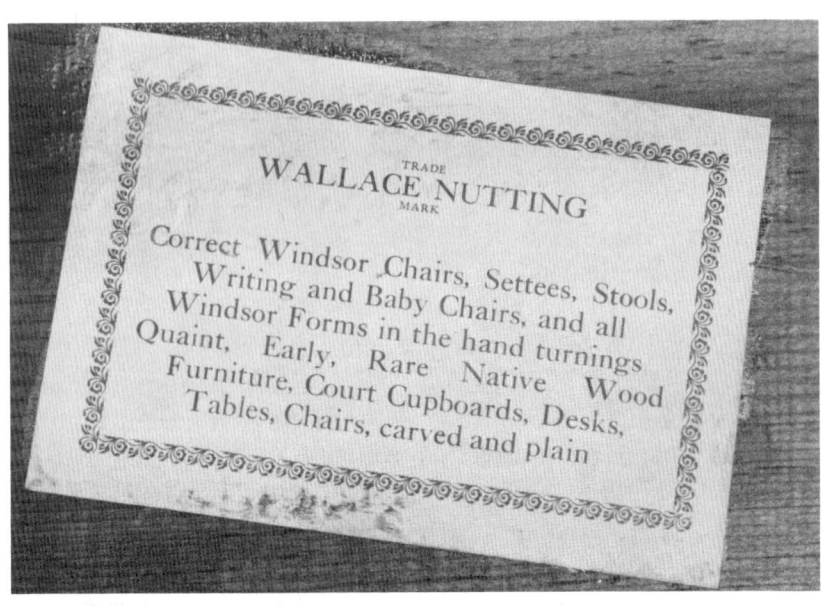

Paper Labels

Chapter 9

Identifying Wallace Nutting Furniture

One question I am frequently asked is "How do I know if I have a piece of Wallace Nutting Furniture?".

In most instances, the answer is quite obvious. Nutting intended to clearly mark all of his furniture...in a manner that no one could miss...for two reasons.

First, Wallace Nutting was proud of his furniture reproductions. His company produced some of the finest furniture of the 20th century and he wanted everyone to know it. Placing his name on each piece served as an excellent form of advertising.

But just as important as the advertising function, Nutting was fearful that unscrupulous people might try to re-sell his reproductions as original, period pieces (something that eventually did happen...many times).

So Nutting went out of his way to clearly identify each piece of his furniture. We've already briefly touched upon the Paper Labels and two types of Branded Signatures in earlier chapters. But in addition to elaborating on these, we'll discuss several other ways you can identify Nutting furniture today.

Paper Labels

The earliest method Nutting used to identify his reproduction furniture was to glue a Paper Label to some inconspicuous location. On Windsor chairs, it was generally on the underside of the seat; on tables it was usually on the underside of the table top or in the drawer; on chests and case pieces it was on the backside, or in, or under, a drawer.

The earliest label, measured approximately 6"x8", was marked **Wallace Nutting Inc, Saugus, Mass**, and contained several paragraphs of sales copy within a value-border design. Over the next few years Nutting used several different Paper Labels, but each had the same purpose: to advertise the piece of furniture as **Wallace Nutting** and to differentiate his reproductions from authentic antiques.

Occasionally Nutting also used a Paper Tag which was affixed to the furniture by means of a thin wire. One such tag read:

> Wallace Nutting
> Furniture
>
> ---
>
> STYLE AND STRENGTH
> All Hand Turned
> All Maple
> Amber Finish
> Mortised and Pinned
> Square Pegs
> In Round Holes.
> Supremacy
> In Reproductions
> A Good Name Is Better
> Than Great Riches
> Name Burned In

One way to determine the approximate date of a piece of Wallace Nutting furniture with a Paper Label is through the address on the Paper Label:

> **Rule of Thumb: You can determine the approximate date of Wallace Nutting furniture through the address on the Paper Label:**
> * Saugus   - 1917-1920
> * Ashland   - 1920-1922
> * Framingham - 1923-1926/27

Script Branded Signature

As we've already mentioned, Nutting sold his business in 1922, along with the right to use the Nutting name. It would appear that all furniture made by the new owners was marked with a distinctive **Script Branded Signature.**

The reason I say "appear" is that I have seen one, and only one, piece of transition furniture marked with a Paper Label. This label was fairly loose, and the possibility exists that someone may have added the label at a later date. However, if this label was original, the possibility exists that the new owners may have used Paper Labels for a very short period of time before changing to the Script Brand. In all my years of collecting, aside from the one piece mentioned above, all transition pieces I have seen were marked with the distinctive Script Brand.

There has also been some speculation that Nutting himself may have initiated the Script Brand just prior to selling the business in 1922. After all, his "script" signature was the trademark of his pictures and, for the sake of consistency, a "script" marking on his

Script Branded Signature

Block Branded Signature

furniture would have made a great deal of sense. The possibility does exist that because of his extreme displeasure with the quality of the transition pieces bearing the Script Branded Signature, Nutting may have been willing to renounce a few of his own "Script" pieces in order to clear his name of all other Script Branded pieces.

But this is nothing more than a theory put forth by several collectors. Neither research compiled by the Wallace Nutting Collector's Club, nor all the research compiled by the late Louis MacKeil, nor any information put forward by anyone else to date, has confirmed that Nutting himself used the Script Branded Signature. And, in the absense of any confirming information that Nutting himself ever used the Script Brand, I feel comfortable offering the following:

> **Rule of Thumb: Furniture marked with the Script Branded Signature was produced between 1922-23 and was made when Nutting did not own the company.**

Block Branded Signatures

One of the first things Nutting did upon resuming control of his company in 1923 was to renounce the Script Branded furniture of his predecessors. Beginning in his 1924 Furniture Catalog, and in future catalogs, Nutting made the following claim:

> My name in plain capitals thus
> **WALLACE NUTTING**
> is burned into every piece I endorse. I will not be responsible for a script letter formerly used as a mark.

Block Branded Signature...Single Line

Block Branded Signature...Double Line

Thus, furniture produced after Nutting re-purchased his company in 1923 is clearly marked with the **Block Branded Signature**. This brand was approximately 1" high, nearly 12" long, and about 1/4" deep. The only way to remove it would be to chisel it out of the wood, leaving an unrepairable gouge that would alert any potential buyer of an 'original' piece.

Sometimes the two names "WALLACE NUTTING" would be on one line; other times the "WALLACE" would be on a separate line above the "NUTTING".

Based upon the number of pieces I have seen with both a Paper Label and a Block Branded Signature, there was probably a period of several years where both markings were used, probably up through 1926 or 1927.

Punched (or Incised) Wallace Nutting Name

Sometimes you may also see the name 'WALLACE NUTTING' **punched** into a piece of furniture. Not to be confused with the much more obvious 'Brand', the name 'WALLACE NUTTING' was literally formed in sharp metal die, and literally punched, or hammered, directly into the wood.

This marking is much smaller than either type of brand, and was generally used where the brand was either inappropriate or would not fit, for example, on the underside of a rear stretcher of a rushed chair, or on the bottom of a small article.

Although this punched marking is more unusual than either the Paper Label and Script or Block Branded Signatures, value is not impacted either positively or negatively. Although most collectors would prefer a Paper Label or Block Branded Signature, the quality and condition of the piece is much more important in determining value than the type of marking used.

Punched Name

I have never seen this form of identification used on a transition piece so its appearance should signify a higher quality item.

Punched (or Incised) Furniture Design Numbers

Over a period of 20 years, Nutting produced more than 500 different furniture designs. Obviously he needed a method of identifying each of these different designs, both within his studio and workshop, and in his sales literature. To accomplish this he developed a series of **Furniture Design Numbers**.

Probably the largest collection of Furniture Design Numbers can be found in the back of the 1930 **Wallace Nutting General Catalog, Supreme Edition**. Here you will see Design Numbers ranging from 1-1000, with each number representing a specific Furniture Design.

These Furniture Design Numbers were further broken down into specific sub-categories:

1-36	Small Articles
34-58c	Finials
59-98	Clocks
101-292	Stools, Signs, High Chairs
301-399c	Side Chairs
401-499c	Arm Chairs
513-599b	Settles, Settees
601-699	Tables, Stands
700-749	Desks
750-777b	Mirrors
801-850b	Beds
900-1000	Cabinet Pieces

Punched Number

It was not uncommon for the Furniture Design Number to be literally punched, or stamped, into the piece. Generally when the Furniture Design Number was included, it was near the Paper Label or the Brand.

How can you use this to your advantage as a collector? Well, we've already talked about Paper Labels being intentionally removed for unscrupulous purposes. But it was also fairly common for the Paper Label to simply fall off over the years. Or sometimes they were intentionally removed by the owner, not unlike removing a label from a pillow or mattress. After all, whoever would have thought (besides Nutting himself) that Wallace Nutting furniture would ever become so collectible.

Anyway, how can this information help you? Once you learn to identify Wallace Nutting furniture by its excellent form, **and** once you understand the Furniture Design Numbering system, you're armed with valuable information unknown by most other collectors.

For example, on more than several occasions I have been at an auction where I saw a piece of Wallace Nutting furniture...with the punched Furniture Design Number, but **without the Paper Label**. Without a Paper Label or Brand, few people in the country are experienced enough to realize its true identity.

So, if you're at an auction where a very nice Pennsylvania Comb Back Windsor Arm Chair is being sold, a chair that that is obviously not period, but a piece that is probably an early 20th century reproduction, the appearance of a punched '412' on the bottom should tip you off to the chair's true identity.

You should be aware that the punched Furniture Design Numbers have been found on both Script and Block Branded pieces so the appearance of a punched Furniture Design Number should not be taken as an absolute sign of quality.

Five Wallace Nutting Catalogs
1924 (u.l.); 1927 (l.l.); 1930 (c.); 1927-28 (u.r.); 1937 (l.r.)

Visual Identification

Although not as precise as the previously mentioned methods, there is a sixth way to identify a piece of Wallace Nutting furniture: **Visual Identification through Wallace Nutting's Reproduction Furniture Catalogs.**

There are undoubtedly pieces of unmarked, unidentified Nutting furniture in circulation. Some of these have lost their Paper Label, have no identifiable Furniture Design Number, and oxidation has removed any evidence of the former label. As we discussed earlier, sometimes Nutting sold his furniture *'in the white'* (unfinished), and whenever Nutting sold a piece of furniture *'in the white'*, it was sold unmarked. And occasionally, especially with pieces having little space available for a large brand (e.g., chairs with rushed seats), Nutting would simply fail to add his name.

So the net effect is that there **are** pieces of unsigned, unmarked Wallace Nutting furniture still in circulation. Some of these are probably being passed over as someone else's 20th century reproductions, and some of them are still being bought, sold, or cherished as authentic antiques.

How do you identify such pieces? As a last resort, in the absence of any distinguishing markings...Paper Label...Script Brand ...Block Brand...Punched Name...or Punched Number...you may be able to refer to one of Nutting's Furniture Catalogs. The most easily available Catalog is the 1930 **Wallace Nutting General Catalog, Supreme Edition,** which has been reprinted and is currently available (see the Inside Title Page opposite the Table of Contents for details on ordering).

In my own collection I also have the 1918 **Windsor Chair Catalog,** the **1924 Furniture Catalog,** the **1927 Furniture, Rugs, and Iron Catalog,** the **1927/28 Furniture Catalog,** and the **1937 Final Edition Furniture Catalog.**

Each of these catalogs can be used to visually identify and authenticate a piece of unmarked Nutting furniture. Early, authentic furniture was hand-made, not machine produced. As a result., each piece was slightly different from the next.

Nutting furniture, on the other hand, was intended to be copied from the Model. Each piece was *intended* to look *exactly* like the Model, and Nutting's craftsmen would be fired if they deviated too far from the Model.

If the piece of furniture you are viewing looks exactly like the comparable piece in the catalog, if the turnings, carvings, and design appears exactly the same, if the measurements from the book correspond to what you are previewing, there is a real good chance the piece you are looking at is a Wallace Nutting reproduction.

The value of the various catalogs lies in the fact that Nutting did not produce all the same designs for twenty years. Some styles were indeed good sellers and he included them in all his catalogs. Other pieces were not produced over that full twenty year period. Some pieces had production difficulties and were dropped from later catalogs, other pieces were not introduced until later years and they will be missing from earlier catalogs, and some pieces were simply dropped because of poor sales.

But, if you are going to obtain just one Furniture Catalog, purchase the 1930 **Wallace Nutting General Catalog, Supreme Edition**. This was his most complete Furniture Catalog and is the only one that has been reproduced and is available at an inexpensive price. (His original Furniture Catalogs today cost more than $100 each, when you can find them).

Another question that frequently arises concerns which type of furniture, the Paper Label or Block Brand, is better. There are really two schools of thought here.

One group believes that all Paper Label furniture is better. They believe that this furniture was the earliest made, and was made with more attention to detail than later furniture. They believe that more time went into each piece, and that Paper Label furniture was less prone to the problems associated with "mass production".

The other group believes that Block Branded furniture is better. They believe that although Paper Label furniture is good, there were more production difficulties with Paper Label furniture (e.g., cracking bows) because it was the earliest furniture produced and was somewhat experimental in nature. These production difficulties were later resolved by the time the Block Branded furniture was produced and this group believes that furniture with the Block Brand is of better quality.

Which theory is correct? The truth probably lies somewhere in the middle. The quality of both were very good. I am aware of collectors who prefer each specific marking if they can get it, but if they are unable to locate the marking of their choice, the other is more than acceptable.

Rule of Thumb, you can generally date Wallace Nutting furniture as follows:

* Paper Label only...1917-1922
* Script Branded Signature...1922-1923
* Block Branded Signature and Paper Label...1923-1926
* Block Branded Signature only...1926-1937

Wallace Nutting - died July 19, 1941

Chapter 10

Recollections of Wallace Nutting

The following narrative was written by William L. Bowers many years ago concerning his association with Wallace Nutting in the late 1930's. This article was originally published in 1974 by **The Antique Trader** (Dubuque, Iowa) who was kind enough to give us permission to reprint the article in its entirety.

Although some of the smallest details are not 100% accurate, most information is generally correct and I think you will agree that it provides a fascinating insight into the inner workings of the Wallace Nutting Furniture Studio, and into the unique personality of Wallace Nutting.

"I had been corresponding with Wallace Nutting perhaps a year or two, before meeting him at Washington and Jefferson College where he received an honorary degree, Doctor of Humanities in 1935.

I plied him regularly with about a letter a week with so many questions about his work. He never ever failed to answer me promptly. I suppose I was his number one fan and first true admirer to receive such consideration.

It all finally culminated in the form of a telegram in the fall 1939, offering me a year's work, at thirty dollars a week. This certainly needed no thought. In less than a week I was off to Framingham to start my new adventure. About a month later I found a place to rent and moved my wife and two small daughters to Massachusetts to join me.

My arrival in Framingham was rather dismal. Fall was well

advanced this far north, and everything looked bleak. I had to see the WN (Wallace Nutting) Studio before anything else. It was back of the Congregation Church on Park Street, in the center of town, and very easy to locate. It was not an object of beauty. A great, gaunt, unpainted, three story, frame building that was at one time a straw hat factory. No trees or shrubbery adorned the outside, not even grass. And this was the place that housed all that beauty? Everything was closed up tightly so I retired to my hotel room for the night. No visions of sugar plums danced through my head!

I was there in the morning to present myself. Apparently WN had done this hiring quietly and on his own, for no one knew who I was or why I was there. The foreman of the cabinet-makers was an understanding man and put a few tools in my hand and said, start in, you may as well-no one else knows what he is doing. From that moment I realized all would be played by ear, plus what you could see. This was right, for at no time were there any hard and fast rules about anything, except starting and quitting work. Everything was run according to how WN felt about the affairs of the day. He did not operate an efficient workshop and would not listen to practical advice, that is, from his foreman and older workers. He was the boss and if it was wrong, he would take the blame.

I could see how things were going and in about six months the big order that brought me up there was filled and then it was all downhill. Several men were laid off, picture business was slow, and furniture sales off the floor were few and far between. The place carried a huge inventory and he kept adding to it, to try and keep his men. At this time there were only six of us working on furniture, two wood finishers upstairs, two or three girls coloring pictures, one photo finisher, and three in the office.

The cabinet shop was on the ground floor, or basement. The worst shop I ever worked in for conditions, poorly lighted and heated, and sanitary conditions, deplorable. No doubt WN had visited shops in foreign countries that were worse and got the idea this somehow made good furniture. He was always quoting how he liked beauty about him, but he never spent much time down there with us. He did not employ a janitor-waste of money, everyone sort of helped, but no one ever cleaned the plumbing fixtures so they were slowly turning green, algae was slowly covering the lavoratory. WN said he hated cheap plumbing fixtures so upstairs he had his own private toilet of marble fixtures, taken from an old hotel in Boston, marble floor and the door was locked, of course, and nobody ever got in there.

The office was in front on the first floor, a great hall leading to the front door separating it from the rest of the floor given over to the picture business. WN had his great flat top desk in the center of the room and used a writing arm Windsor to work on. The desk was piled high with his books and brochures, and catalogues. When the northeasters blew and rattled the building, the temperature generally fell to about 55-60 degrees. Then WN would wrap a huge muffler about his neck and put his hat on, calmly cutting his nails with a huge pair of tailor shears with which he opened mail. Esther Svensen was always afraid he would injure himself with these, but he never did.

Ernest Donnelly, his right-hand man and invaluable asset in all ways, kept the whole ship from sinking by his constant watchfulness and guidance. At one time Ernest told me the treasury was almost down to nothing. WN replied "providence will provide." Well, long about March or April, providence didn't show up and everybody was laid off except me. I had a written contract and took a job as night watchman there. Things didn't get any better to speak of, times were still tight, so about the end of June, 1940, I gave up and returned to Chambersburg, Pa. I felt I had accomplished what I went for, in that WN let me copy most of his patterns and furniture pictures. So in reality, I brought the WN furniture business back to Chambersburg, on paper that is.

We still corresponded until his death in July 1941. WN always said he was going to leave the business to his employees, as neither he nor Mrs. Nutting had any close relatives left. He left everything to his wife and her discretion. She gave the picture business to Ernest Donnelly and Esther Swenson, the two oldest and most trusted employees. They didn't have the capital to find new quarters, etc., so sold it to a Mr. Currier in Boston, one of their retailers of pictures there. I suppose he got the negatives also, but never heard what he did with them nor did I ever see anymore pictures made, or for sale. The rights to make WN furniture were sold to Drexel Furniture Company who planned a line of WN pieces. They abandoned it as too costly and I never heard anything more. **The Furniture Treasury** *was sold to the present publishers. WN's antique collection, what was left of it, sold at Parke Bernet Galleries in New York in 1942, things bringing only a fraction of their present worth. At Mrs. Nutting's death in September, 1944 all went to her pet charity, Berea College, in Kentucky for distressed mountain folk.*

Mrs. Nutting was a kindly, generous woman, very small and bird-like, really gracious. It was she that gave the employees Christmas gifts, for she had a kind heart. WN scoffed at this gesture as he deemed this "both humiliating to giver and receiver." She loved gardening and had a beautiful place up at Framingham Center, where they lived and which they called "Nuttingholme." A Mr. Kelly worked for her full time and did the driving. WN never had anything nice to say about Mr. Kelly. Mrs. Nutting was the one that designed, and had made the rugs that were sold by the mountain people she was interested in, down in Kentucky. She had a loom there at the house and gave it what time she could, but her interests were so varied, especially in the summer with the garden. WN took many pictures in her garden. Nuttingholme was also a surprise when I first saw it. A great old Victorian mansion with everything about out of taste according to WN's precepts of beauty. I judged that this was Mrs. Nutting's home and if Wallace didn't like it, he could stay at the studio; he was there most of his time anyhow. Never the less, it was a quiet, dignified, place and at their time of life they didn't want anymore projects. After all, WN had bought and furnished some six or eight places for his furniture and pictures so no doubt felt he had done about everything.

Wallace Nutting was not well liked by the townspeople. Of course they didn't understand him and his search for beauty. And furthermore he said it was too late in the day to change them. He had an aloof attitude toward the employees, those that didn't understand him didn't stay long. One had to see things his way or there was no room. Of course, I was top of the class, being so devoted, along with Ernest Donnelly and Miss Svenson. It was odd how the other employees treated me, nothing malicious, but very watchful and secretive as if WN and I were partners. I can understand their distrust in a way, as many a time he would take me from the shop on a picture taking trip, or to Boston antiquing. I got to meet the best dealers in Boston and see a lot of fine things. I remember one old time dealer up on Beacon Hill who had a shop and remarked to me on the side one day "I knew him, way back when he wasn't so holy." There may be something to this as WN liked to tell of a picture circulated of him in his ministerial days, showing him seated with a strumpet (i.e., prostitute) on his lap. Of course, said he, someone superimposed his head on someone else's shoulders in making the picture. Occasionally he filled a pulpit as a guest and took me along on Sunday. He spoke well and very commandingly, never at a loss for words or ideas.

It is good things turned out as they did for as my wife said at one time-"this is all too much Wallace Nutting and no time for me." And I couldn't afford a gardner like Mr. Kelly.

I also remember going along several times on trips to take pictures. I was impressed in that he worked quickly and with confidence that the results would be exactly what he wanted. Always sure of himself.

Wallace Nutting was quite deaf, but considered this an asset. It *certainly served as an excuse to ignore people and unpleasant situations. He had a hearing-aid, but most of the time I doubt if it was turned on, because generally he spoke in a booming manner. Many of his personal affairs were conducted behind a screen in the office, a small narrow room with thin partitions and lined with filing cabinets. One day his physician called and they retired back of the screen. It seems WN had a problem, as he told the doctor, he was bothered with youthfulness and needed some advice. As the doctor spoke rather low, no one ever learned the remedy. WN at one time told Ernest Donnelly he wished his people would come to him for advice with their problems. Little did he know how quickly and thoroughly he was watched, and that his problems were theirs, really. Even his waste basket was gone through well, before being burned. Everybody in the whole building was just plain nosey, or rather their own life was so drab they rode on his coat tails for the interest he generated. None of them ever thought of doing anything on their own, without being told how. He knew this and remarked they would all be paupers if it weren't for him.*

No one ever really knew Wallace Nutting as he presented a formidable figure of politeness and reserve. However, he had a humorous side and could enjoy a joke or situation. He tried to present a father image to his employees, but it didn't work out. They knew his promises were made on sunny days and not dependable. He relied heavily on his bad memory, old age, and being tired. One old employee, George Sturgen, the Windsor chair maker was WN's pet workman. He was a workhorse, spent hours over his regular time, was dependable, and everything you would want. He was the first to be laid off. I heard WN say that he would go hungry before laying off George, but he loved to say things like that and always gave a little smile.

We had a wood turner that did the legs and spindles on the furniture, and George bent the hoops in a steam chest, shaped the seats by hand, bored the holes properly for the parts, and then assembled the piece. The finishers took care of it from there.

George usually put up two dozen at a time, of course depending on orders, but at this time the stock was heavy. They would sell one chair, and make five more. The back arm bows with the knuckle termination were made ahead so the wood carver could do these before being assembled.

The best cabinet maker was a Swede, Ernest Gerstan, a small, wiry man that moved fast. He was the best joiner I ever knew; his work was perfect. I learned a great deal from him. On the other side of me was Joe Babrunos, from Riga, Latvia. He was a heavy, ponderous man that moved slowly, but precisely; a fine workman, but slow and from the old school. He told me he served his time in Moscow and often spoke of the Cossacks in a hushed voice as a most dreaded and feared group. That was under the old Czar and a way of life he knew as a young man in Russia before the Revolution. He came to America before the first World War with that big flood of immigration. Wallace Nutting mentioned there were more foreign born people in Boston than what remained of the Old New England stock.

Mr. Johnson, the wood carver, had a small shop in Cambridge and called for and delivered his work as needed. He was from Sweden, a very fine workman the best WN ever had. He could carve almost as fast as a machine, improvising with his feelings as he went along. He was not a mechanical carver, as most are, that just repeats a thing monotonously.

Wallace Nelson was a good mechanic and was shop foreman. He was WN's right hand man there and WN relied on his judgement to produce what he wanted. Nelson was from Canada, French I think, a small man that spent a lot of time not working. He was capable all right, but Wallace Nutting did make his life difficult, especially when things didn't go well. There were several other men that were good workmen, but nothing remarkable about them.

The finishing room was on the third floor. Two men were there most of the time, nothing but shellac was used, each piece taking between six and nine applications and then was hand rubbed. If it was to be stained, this step was first. The amount of time on the finish was approximately a third or half of the building time. At the time I was there, fine cabinet woods like Cuban mahogany were still available and used exclusively. It seemed a shame to cover up such quality with a lot of finish, but that was the taste of the time.

Wallace Nutting did not make any money on his furniture, perhaps at the best of times he did, but over all, it was the picture business that carried it all along. Mr. Donnelly told me that between 1926-29 they sold about a thousand dollars worth of photos a day and also turned out a lot of furniture, having about thirty employees then. It all came to sudden stop with the stock market crash in 1929. WN had a very large collection of antiques then, most of it from the furnishings of his houses. This was sold to John Wannamaker in New York who put out a catalogue and merchandized it in the arts magazine. For the next ten or twelve years it was mighty rough going to keep things up to Wallace Nutting standards and ideals. Too bad he died then, for in another two years he would have seen better conditions and a great demand for his furniture. The picture business, however, never regained its popularity, color photography and cheap color prints taking over by this time.

As far as I know Drexel never did anything more with the Wallace Nutting furniture line, nor did anymore pictures appear. Mr. Donnelly moved into Boston and tried a line of miniature paintings and silhouettes with his old picture customers, but it didn't turn out very well so he moved to Philadelphia to work for David Stockwell in the antique business. Donnelly left him in 1970 to retire to Ireland where he died of a heart attack in the fall of 1973.

Esther Swenson never did anything more when she retired from WN's in 1944. I know she had a great deal of information and momentos as she was there the longest of all, but I do not know what happened to these.

One might say WN contributed more for the preservation of our past heritage of American arts and culture than anyone else. We had greater names in the arts, but they reached selected few. Wallace Nutting was for everybody and everyone appreciated him. He put everything he had, both finances and all his time, to explain how and why our ancestors lived and felt.

Our great museums, and names like Henry DuPont at Winterthur, are unquestionably the epitome of quality and taste-but these are the results of many millions of dollars and the employment of well-trained personnel. Our best institutions are the sum total of many people working at it full time and having unlimited amounts of money. Wallace Nutting did all this first, and single-handedly. It took a lot of judgement, foresight and study to determine what was the best, before there were any guidelines in books or pictures. We had a few good names about this time that WN thought a lot of and consulted such as Henry Wood Erving, J. Stodgell Stokes, and of course, the best dealers at that time. He knew them all well.

When H. F. DuPont was first forming his great collection Wallace Nutting was invited down to view his things. Nutting must have made severe criticism as he was never asked again, or consulted, or ever quoted in their writings or publications.

I spent a lot of time with Mr. Donnelly as we were about the closest to WN and really the most interested in him. There were always new antidotes for me about WN, even things that had happened long ago, like the time WN lost control of his car, mounted the sidewalk, and struck a store front in Sudbury. Neither of them was seriously hurt, but quite shaken up. Another time WN bought a court cupboard from a woman and she sued him to return it, claiming he underpaid her. They took it to court and WN won the case by proving he paid her more than anyone else on record at that time for a similar item. It was all in the papers and some say it wasn't good for his reputation. WN never ever listened to advice- he did the deciding. As he once said, "I'll even pay to be wrong." I suppose he found a lot of satisfaction doing just what he wanted. This is what upset the management of the business. They would have things going well, and WN would upset all for no reason at all, perhaps some foolish whim to which no thought was given.

When things were going wrong or there was some sort of crisis at the shop, WN disappeared for a few days till it blew over, Mr. Donnelly taking charge. One time there was no money to meet the payroll, so WN left instructions to give each employee a piece of furniture. A few took it, but most others had to have money and Mr. Donnelly paid them from his funds. Later WN reimbursed him.

Quoting the last letter I received from WN, in the spring of 1941, he says "It is really old age that compels me to quit. I am so tired and no longer able to cope with the increasing problems of business." The fun and challenge had gone from his work, as the times demanded stricter attention to business, as government controls and interference made it impossible to do things the old way.

I suppose he died a satisfied but saddened man, as the world was changing and he was too tired to start over. However, he did not give up, but was at the studio everyday, even if it was only for a few hours. He was only ill a few days at home before his death.

A word about the actual making of his furniture. One or two men did the mill work on the lumber, processing it to correct size and put it at the workman's bench. Here, the hand-work started such as dovetailing parts together, and assembling the whole according to the patterns. The completed piece was finished by hand- scraping, very little sandpaper being used. Nothing was glued up to make a thick piece. Only solid planks of full thickness were used, such as on the block front pieces which required a plank three inches thick to saw out the required shape.

The cabinetmaker carried out the entire job or piece, so it was the product of one man, with the exception of the finish and applying the hardware. The hardware was supplied by William Ball, Sr. of West Chester, Penna. according to WN's specifications. The fine Cuban mahogany was bought in Boston from Palmer and Parker, imported lumber dealers. They are the ones that supplied WN with a French walnut plant 6" thick, 30" wide and 16 feet long for the library table legs on the Andover Academy job. Nutting made four of these tables for the school, in the 17th century style. In the early 1920's furniture of the Pilgrim Century was much in demand. That is, oak court cupboards, Hadley Chests, Brewster Chairs and early William and Mary looking glasses. Also, gate leg tables and slat back chairs were much in demand. The public taste began to change about 1928 to walnut and mahogany pieces of the better type. The earlier style never revived and is still a slow seller today. Even the antique pieces don't bring near the old prices of the 1920's.

Mr. Nutting had a blacksmith working over at Saugus. He was an Italian and a superb workman, fashioning the most delicate items on his anvil. WN complained that he always smelled of wine. The demand for iron objects ceased with no new building and he gave up supporting the venture.

Volume three of the Furniture Treasury is a monumental work of Ernest Donnelly in that the drawings are all his free-hand sketching, requiring countless hours to complete. They were all copied from photographs of original pieces. It was quite a task to ascertain correct proportions, not to mention perspective, which was most important. Donnelly also worked up a line of silhouettes that emphasized furniture details. These did not sell too well.

I feel that everyone that worked with WN never regretted a minute of it. Everyone came in each day with the expectation of WN confounding them with some new project or idea. "

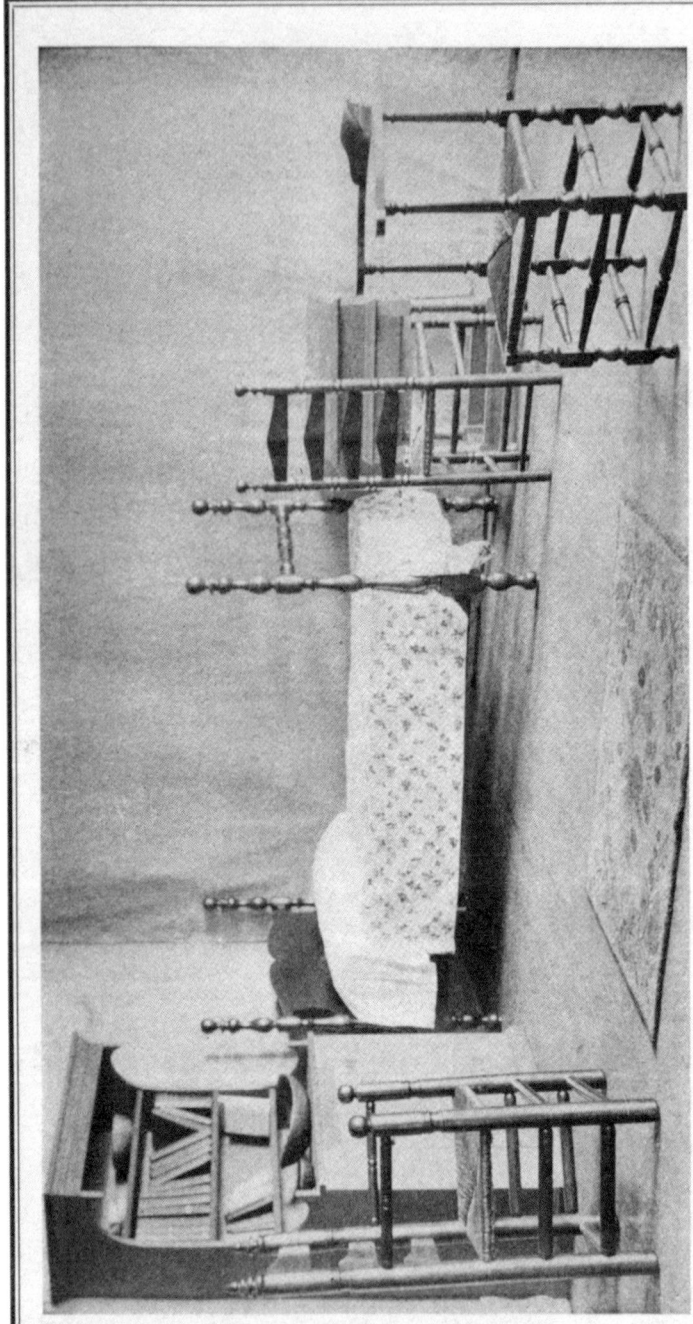

Antiques, July, 1929

Chapter 11

Wallace Nutting Advertising

It should be clear by now that one of the keys to Wallace Nutting's success was his ability to **market** his products. There were other photographers selling hand-colored pictures throughout New England, but none marketed them as effectively as Nutting.

Other individuals published furniture books, but none sold more than Nutting.

And others were reproducing furniture in the early 20th century, but none were more aggressive marketers than Nutting.

Nutting seems to have written most, if not all, of his advertising copy. His flowery prose and inability to sound humble were truely Nutting trademarks. He sincerely believed that he produced the finest furniture anywhere...and he had no reservations about telling the world about it.

His furniture catalogs were an excellent form of advertising but they reached relatively few people. In order to more aggressively market his products, Nutting made extensive use of space advertising. Although he did a limited amount of advertising in various local and regional publications, most of his advertising dollars were spent in **The Magazine Antiques.**

That one magazine enabled him to cost effectively reach the segment of the American population most likely to purchase his furniture: upscale households with an intense interest in the finest form of early American antiques...and the financial resources with which to buy them.

These pages will give you an indication of the type of products Wallace Nutting advertised...and the image he presented.

A handsome copy of a Duncan Phyfe dining table, in heavy Cuban mahogany. It is also made in two parts.

One of six hundred fine copies

Specialty of twin beds in many patterns

WALLACE NUTTING
46 Park Street
Framingham, Massachusetts
Rich catalogue, $2.00
MONEY REFUNDED ON FIRST PURCHASE

Antiques, September, 1937

A Copy of a Splendid Example from the Savery School

The incised and the applied carving covers the full length of the skirt. The corners are cut in the conventional clover leaf design. Richly carved knees and quarter columns. Heavy Cuban mahogany. The highboy to match is also in stock.

One of six hundred fine copies — Specialty of twin beds in many patterns

WALLACE NUTTING
46 Park Street, Framingham, Massachusetts
Rich catalog, $2.00   Money refunded on first purchase

Antiques, August, 1940

The most beautiful, best made, most correct, general purpose Windsor chair. Seat in one piece deeply scooped. One of forty varieties. Hundreds of cabinets and other pieces

■

Many antiques for sale, bought to copy.

■

Catalog $1.00.
Vol. III
FURNITURE
TREASURY
$8.00

WALLACE NUTTING

46 PARK STREET, SO. FRAMINGHAM, MASS., *Back of Post Office*

Antiques, April, 1940

WALLACE NUTTING

46 Park Street
Framingham, Massachusetts

(Two miles south of Framingham Center traffic light)

◇

Mr. Nutting started on an unique enterprise. It was to make a perfect reproduction of every good design in furniture, at least one style each, from 1620 to 1830. This aim so ambitious was achieved this year.

It was a remarkable opportunity for the public. Such a thing was never tried before. Having accomplished this, Mr. Nutting, in his 80th year, is retiring from furnituremaking, and his picture work will be continued by him for his associates.

The hundred thousand dollar stock, many being unique pieces, will be offered where they are, till October 1st, and any balance stored. This is the one "must" among New England visiting points this season.

Antiques, May, 1941 (2 months before his death)

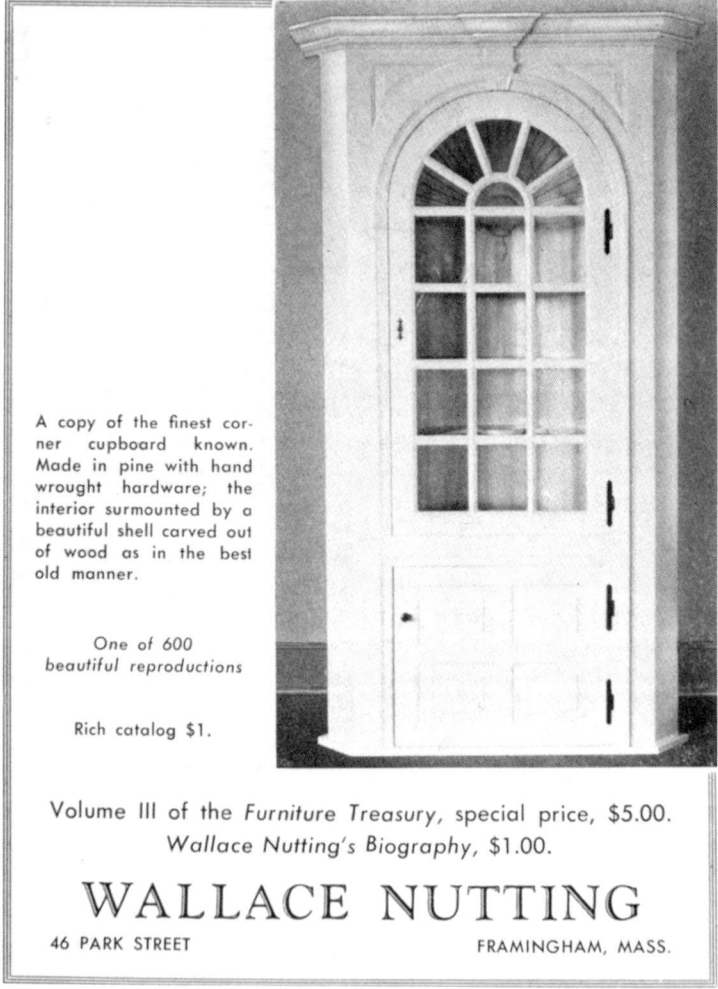

Antiques, February, 1943
Mrs. Nutting was still selling furniture after Nutting's death in 1941

A beautiful mahogany chest of drawers. One of the simplest examples of the Goddard style. Heavy Cuban mahogany in three inch thickness used for the drawers. One of six hundred beautiful reproductions.

Volume III, FURNITURE TREASURY, 1000 drawings of details and plentiful instructions, $8.

Catalog of furniture reproductions, $1

GREAT SUMMER EXHIBIT, OPEN SATURDAYS

WALLACE NUTTING
46 Park Street   So. Framingham, Mass.

Antiques, August, 1940

One of our most popular beds. In unfailing demand. Only the heavy Cuban mahogany is used in our pieces where this wood is called for.

WALLACE NUTTING
46 PARK STREET
FRAMINGHAM, MASSACHUSETTS
RICH CATALOG, $1.00
Volume III Furniture Treasury, 1000 drawings, $8

Antiques, August, 1941

Chapter 12

Listing of Recent Sale Prices

As stated in the **Introduction** of this book, **The Guide to Wallace Nutting Furniture** is not, nor is it intended to be, a 'Price Guide'. There is simply not enough documentable pricing information available to develop standardized price ranges for each individual category of Wallace Nutting furniture.

But that doesn't mean there isn't any pricing information available. I've been monitoring the prices of Wallace Nutting furniture sales for many years, trying to stay abreast of what was coming into the marketplace...and what it was selling for.

The prices contained in this section come from many different sources, including:

* Furniture sold at our Wallace Nutting Auctions since 9/88
* Furniture sold at Skinner's Wallace Nutting Auction (4/89)
* Auction and Show results printed in such trade papers as **Maine Antique Digest; Antiques & Auction Weekly (The Bee); Mass. Bay Antiques; The Antique Trader; (Ohio) Antique Review; New England Antiques Journal; Mid-Atlantic Antiques Magazine; Antique & Auction News; Collectors News; Southern Antiques; Antique Gazette; New York-Penn Collector; New York Antique Almanac; Antiques and Collecting Hobbies,** just to name a few
* Wallace Nutting furniture advertised in the above papers
* Wallace Nutting furniture I have seen at antique shows
* Private Sales of Wallace Nutting furniture
* Prices reported in the Wallace Nutting Collector's Club News Letters
* Letters I have received from owners of Wallace Nutting furniture from around the country

All prices included here date from 9/88-7/90. Most represent final sale prices, where they were obtainable. If the final sale price was unobtainable, I included the asking price where I felt it to be reasonable and consistent with the quality and rarity of the piece.

It should be understood that most prices included here represent **Retail Prices**. If you are looking to **sell** a piece of Wallace Nutting furniture, remember that dealers must make a fair profit and expect them to offer proportionately less than retail.

You must also understand that not all prices here reflect the absolute value. As in any auction environment, only some items sell for their true value; many sell for considerably less than their true retail value, while others sell for well above their actual worth.

Anyway, until more detailed and extensive pricing information becomes available, this information represents a good starting point for determining the approximate value of a piece of Wallace Nutting furniture.

Type	#	Item	Where	Amount
Arm Chair	n/k	Chippendale	Auction	$525
Arm Chair	401	Windsor Continuous Arm	Auction	$350
Arm Chair	401	Windsor, Continuous Arm	Auction	$660
Arm Chair	401	Windsor Continuous Arm	Show	$795
Arm Chair	401	Windsor Continuous Arm	Auction	$875
Arm Chair	401	Windsor Continuous Arm	Show	$895
Arm Chair	401	Windsor Continuous Arm	Auction	$1,100
Arm Chair	401	Windsor Continuous Arm	Auction	$1,475
Arm Chair	408	Windsor Knuckle Arm,	Auction	$525
Arm Chair	411	Brewster	Private	$1,800
Arm Chair	412	Windsor, Penn. Comb Back	Auction	$1,275
Arm Chair	412	Windsor, Penn. Comb Back	Private	$1,400
Arm Chair	412	Windsor, Penn. Comb Back	Private	$1,600
Arm Chair	412	Windsor, Penn. Comb Back	Auction	$1,760
Arm Chair	412	Windsor, Penn. Comb Back	Show	$2,200
Arm Chair	415	Windsor Comb Back	Auction	$1,125
Arm Chair	415	Windsor Comb Back	Auction	$1,275
Arm Chair	415	Windsor Comb Back	Private	$1,500
Arm Chair	415	Knuckle Arm Comb Back	Show	$1,500
Arm Chair	415	Windsor Comb Back	Auction	$1,725
Arm Chair	416	Pine Settle	Auction	$330
Arm Chair	419	Windsor Double Comb Back	Auction	$770
Arm Chair	419	Windsor Double Comb Back	Auction	$1,100
Arm Chair	419	Windsor Double Comb Back	Auction	$1,350
Arm Chair	419	Windsor Double Comb Back	Private	$1,550
Arm Chair	419	Windsor Double Comb Back	Show	$1,800
Arm Chair	422	Tenon Fan Back	Show	$1,250
Arm Chair	430	Corner	Auction	$375
Arm Chair	430	Corner	Show	$775
Arm Chair	438	Hepplewhite	Private	$1,200
Arm Chair	451	Writing Arm Windsor	Private	$1,500
Arm Chair	451	Writing Arm Windsor	Private	$2,250
Arm Chair	451	Writing Arm Windsor	Private	$2,500
Arm Chair	464	Carver	Private	$1,450
Arm Chair	466	Chippendale Wing	Auction	$1,600
Arm Chair	480	Spanish Footed	Auction	$935
Arm Chair	480	Spanish Footed	Private	$1,200
Arm Chair	490	5-Back Ladderback	Private	$1,100
Arm Chair	492	New England 4-Back	Auction	$585
Arm Chair	492	4 Back Ladderback	Show	$900
Arm Chair	493	Pilgrim 3-Back	Auction	$715
Arm Chair	493	Pilgrim	Private	$1,250

Arm Chair		493	Pilgrim	Private	$1,500
Arm Chair		495	Office	Auction	$360
Bed		809	Low Urn Post	Auction	$385
Bed		811	Brewster	Auction	$675
Bed		811	Brewster	Auction	$775
Bed		811	Brewster (2 Beds)	Auction	$825
Bed		811	Brewster	Auction	$825
Bed		828	Day Bed	Private	$2,600
Bed		832	Federal Tester	Auction	$1,760
Bed		846	Sheraton, 4-Poster	Auction	$2,310
Cabinet Piece		903	Spoon Rack	Auction	$190
Cabinet Piece		909	Chest One Drawer	Auction	$770
Cabinet Piece		909	Chest, One Drawer	Auction	$2,585
Cabinet Piece		909	Chest, One Drawer	Show	$2,850
Cabinet Piece		909	Chest, One Drawer	Auction	$3,200
Cabinet Piece		909	Chest, One Drawer	Private	$4,000
Cabinet Piece		913	Chest of Drawers	Private	$2,600
Cabinet Piece		918	Bureau, Chippendale, Block Front	Auction	$2,200
Cabinet Piece		922	Dresser, Welsh	Private	$3,250
Cabinet Piece		927	Cupboard, Book Case	Auction	$1,265
Cabinet Piece		927	Cupboard, Book Case	Show	$2,200
Cabinet Piece		927	Cupboard, Book Case	Private	$2,800
Cabinet Piece		931	Chest, Sunflower, 2 Drawer	Private	$4,800
Cabinet Piece		931	Chest, Sunflower, 2 Drawer	Auction	$5,775
Cabinet Piece		979	Chest of Drawers, Block & Shell	Auction	$4,400
Cabinet Piece		979	Chest of Drawers, Block & Shell	Auction	$5,280

*** Auction Record ***

Chairs		301/415	Windsor Chairs, Set of 8, (6 Side, 2 Arm), Original Paint	Auction	$15,950
Desk		n/k	Desk, Child's	Auction	$605
Desk		701	Desk, Drop Front	Auction	$1,600
Desk		701	Desk, Drop Front	Auction	$2,500
Desk		729	Desk, Chippendale Slant Front	Auction	$3,520
Desk		729	Secretary, Chippendale	Auction	$6,600

Mirror	755	Walnut with Picture	Show	$275
Mirror	764	Queen Anne with Gold Bird	Show	$900
Mirror	764	Queen Anne with Gold Bird	Private	$1,100
Mirror	764	Chippendale with Gilded Bird	Auction	$1,210
Mirror	766	Chippendale	Auction	$1,540
Mirror	769	Hepplewhite	Auction	$2,800
Mirror	774	Walnut	Private	$750
Misc.	1210	Wig Stand, Chippendale	Auction	$1,210
Settle, Settee	290	Bench, William & Mary	Auction	$525
Settle, Settee	502	Settee, Double Bowback, 6 Legs	Auction	$2,970
Settee, Settle	513	Settle, Two Panel Back	Show	$1,350
Settle, Settee	525	Sofa, Chippendale	Auction	$660
Settee, Settle	533	Settee, Penn. 10 Leg Low Back	Private	$5,500
Settee, Settle	539	Sofa, Sheraton	Private	$1,200
Settee, Settle	589	Settle, Waincot	Private	$1,000
Settee, Settle	594	Settee, Winds. Comb Back 10-Legger	Private	$3,250
Side Chair	301	Windsor Bow Back	Auction	$330
Side Chair	301	Windsor Bow Back	Auction	$475
Side Chair	301	Windsor Bow Back	Show	$475
Side Chair	301	Windsor Bow Back	Auction	$500
Side Chair	301	Windsor Bow Back	Private	$525
Side Chair	301	Windsor Bow Back	Auction	$550
Side Chair	301	Windsor Bow Back	Show	$625
Side Chair	301	Windsor Bow Back	Auction	$675
Side Chair	302	Windsor Bow Back	Auction	$425
Side Chair	302	Windsor Bow Back	Private	$425
Side Chair	302	Windsor Bow Back	Show	$475
Side Chair	302	Windsor Bow Back	Auction	$500
Side Chair	302	Windsor Bow Back	Show	$550
Side Chair	302	Windsor Bow Back	Auction	$575
Side Chair	302	Windsor Bow Back (6)	Auction	$900
Side Chair	310	Windsor Bowback with Brace	Auction	$550
Side Chair	310	Windsor Fan Back	Show	$725
Side Chair	310	Windsor Fan Back	Show	$750
Side Chair	310	Windsor Fan Back	Auction	$850
Side Chair	311	Imposed Comb	Auction	$495
Side Chair	311	Imposed Comb	Show	$825
Side Chair	326	Fan Back with Brace	Show	$725
Side Chair	327	Windsor Fan Back	Auction	$550
Side Chair	329	Windsor Swivel	Auction	$625

Side Chair	329	Windsor Swivel	Auction	$650
Side Chair	329	Windsor Swivel	Show	$775
Side Chair	338	Hepplewhite (Set of 4)	Private	$3,000
Side Chair	349	Windsor Slipper	Auction	$415
Side Chair	349	Windsor Slipper	Private	$525
Side Chair	349	Windsor Slipper	Show	$575
Side Chair	361	Dutch	Auction	$440
Side Chair	374	3-Back Ladderback	Show	$425
Side Chair	380	Spanish Footed	Private	$800
Side Chair	390	5-Back Ladderback	Private	$575
Side Chair	390	5-Back Ladderback	Private	$725
Side Chair	391	6-Back Delaware Valley	Private	$1,100
Side Chair	392	New England Ladderback,	Auction	$525
Side Chair	392	4 Back Ladder Back	Show	$675
Side Chair	392	New England Ladderback,	Auction	$725
Side Chair	392	New England Ladderback, Set of 4	Auction	$1,715
Side Chair	399	Queen Anne, Set of 4	Auction	$2,090
Side Chair	468	Chippendale Wing Back	Auction	$880
Small Article	17	Stand, Windsor Candlestand	Private	$375
Small Article	17	Stand, Windsor Candlestand	Auction	$410
Small Article	17	Stand, Windsor Candlestand	Show	$475
Small Article	17	Stand, Windsor Candlestand	Auction	$500
Small Article	17	Stand, Windsor Candlestand	Private	$525
Small Article	17	Stand, Windsor Candlestand	Auction	$575
Small Article	21	Candlestand, Whirling	Show	$775
Small Article	27	Treen, Salt Dish	Private	$200
Small Article	27	Treen, Salt Dish	Auction	$275
Small Article	27	Treen, Salt Dish	Private	$325
Small Article	30	Treen, Dish	Private	$175
Small Article	40	Hat Rack, Spinning Wheel Type	Auction	$400
Small Article	40	Hat Rack, Spinning Wheel Type	Auction	$400
Small Article	40	Hat Rack, Spinning Wheel Type	Private	$500
Stool	n/k	Child's Windsor Cont. Arm Chair	Auction	$775
Stool	101	Stool	Show	$195
Stool	101	Stool	Private	$250
Stool	102	Stool	Show	$275
Stool	110	Stool	Private	$195
Stool	110	Stool	Show	$325
Stool	145	Windsor Style	Auction	$230
Stool	145	Windsor Style	Auction	$425
Stool	145	Windsor Style	Auction	$475
Stool	145	Windsor Style	Show	$525

Stool		163	Long Stool	Show	$750
Stool		165	Joined, 15"	Show	$475
Stool		165	Joined, 15"	Auction	$550
Stool		166	William & Mary, 15"	Auction	$275
Stool		166	William & Mary, 15"	Show	$425
Stool		169	30" William & Mary	Show	$495
Stool		211	Child's Winds. Comb Back Arm Chair	Auction	$750
Stool		292	Gothic	Show	$275
Stool		292	Gothic	Show	$295
Stool		292	Gothic	Show	$325
Table, Stand	n/k	Table, (Tea Table with Tray)	Auction	$660
Table, Stand	601	Table, Refractory Table	Private	$1,200
Table, Stand	605	Table, 3-Leg Windsor Type	Auction	$320
Table, Stand	605	Table, 3-Leg Windsor Type	Show	$474
Table, Stand	605	Table, 3-Leg Windsor Type	Show	$500
Table, Stand	605	Table, 3-Leg Windsor Type	Show	$575
Table, Stand	608	Stand, Federal	Auction	$440
Table, Stand	610	Table, (Trestle Table)	Auction	$550
Table, Stand	613	Table, Tavern	Auction	$825
Table, Stand	615	Table, Trestle	Auction	$825
Table, Stand	615	Table, Trestle	Show	$1,100
Table, Stand	615	Table, Trestle	Private	$1,200
Table, Stand	615	Table, Trestle	Auction	$1,250
Table, Stand	616	Table, Tuckaway Gateleg	Private	$475
Table, Stand	621	Table, Gateleg	Auction	$385
Table, Stand	621	Table, Gateleg	Auction	$990
Table, Stand	621	Table, Gateleg	Private	$1,200
Table, Stand	621	Table, Gateleg	Show	$1,500
Table, Stand	621	Table, Gateleg	Show	$2,500
Table, Stand	624	Table (Butterfly), William & Mary	Auction	$605
Table, Stand	624	Table, Butterfly	Auction	$605
Table, Stand	624	Table, Butterfly	Private	$675
Table, Stand	624	Table, Butterfly	Show	$795
Table, Stand	637	Table, Library Table	Auction	$825
Table, Stand	637	Table, Library Table	Show	$1,400
Table, Stand	644	Candlestand, Hepplewhite	Auction	$660
Table, Stand	653	Table, William & Mary	Auction	$220
Table, Stand	653	Table, William & Mary	Show	$650
Table, Stand	653	Table, William & Mary	Auction	$750
Table, Stand	660	Table, Tavern Table	Show	$725
Table, Stand	660	Table, (Tavern)	Auction	$770
Table, Stand	660	Table, Tavern	Show	$1,250

Tenoned Fan Back Windsor Arm Chair
New England Turnings, #422

Chapter 13

Conclusion

If someone were to ask me whether they should purchase an authentic American antique or a Wallace Nutting reproduction of comparable form and condition, I would without hesitation recommend the authentic antique... *if they could afford it*. The authentic American antique in excellent condition undoubtedly represents a true piece of Americana and will most likely prove to be an excellent long-term investment.

Unfortunately, most people cannot afford the finest authentic antiques at today's high prices. When the most desirable paintings start bringing over $50,000,000 with increasing regularity...when the finest forms of early American furniture break the $12,000,000 barrier...when the finest pieces in nearly all areas of antiques and collectibles seem to reach record highs on a weekly basis...the other remaining great pieces seem to trickle up in price...beyond the means of all but the wealthiest collectors.

This leaves most collectors two choices:

> a) They can collect authentic antiques that have less than excellent form and design...or antiques that have been repaired or restored over the years. **Or...**
>
> b) They can collect top quality 20th century reproductions which make up for their lack of age with fine lines and correct proportions.

If someone were to ask me whether I would prefer to own a Wallace Nutting reproduction...or an authentic antique that has been repaired and restored...or an authentic antique with less than desirable form and design...I would select the Wallace Nutting reproduction for the following reasons:

1) Wallace Nutting reproductions offer the finest in form and design. Nutting copied the finest styles and designs ever produced by classical American furniture makers. Most of the originals he copied can only be found in museums or private collections today. If I am unable to own the finest authentic antique, I would prefer to own the finest reproduction rather than a second-rate authentic antique.

2) The high quality that Wallace Nutting achieved in his reproductions would be extremely difficult to duplicate today. The primary reason Nutting went out of business was because he lost money making his furniture. He worked with the finest woods, he employed the same techniques used by 17th & 18th century furniture makers, and he didn't cut corners. What furniture maker or furniture company today can operate at a loss for twenty years simply to abide by their personal commitment of creating the finest furniture they are capable of producing?

The same woods and construction techniques that have enabled 17th century furniture to last into the 20th century...will allow Wallace Nutting furniture to remain with us well into the 21st and 22nd centuries, and most likely, beyond.

3) No more Wallace Nutting furniture will ever be produced. There is only a limited amount of Wallace Nutting furniture in existence. In total he reproduced more than 500 different designs. Certain items were produced on a large scale, other designs saw only 4-5 total pieces produced, and still other designs never made it beyond the Model stage. Over the years, a great deal of the furniture has been lost, damaged, or destroyed. What remains will become even more valuable.

4) Wallace Nutting furniture will stand up to daily wear and usage. If you were to spend $10,000, $20,000, or more on an authentic Windsor chair, how often would you use it?

If you were to spend only $2500-$5000 on a set of Nutting chairs, you could feel much more comfortable about using that set, if not on a daily basis, then at least in a more formal, entertaining-type setting.

5) Prices for Wallace Nutting furniture are still quite reasonable for the quality you are getting. Wallace Nutting furniture is not inexpensive today, but neither was it inexpensive when first sold in the 1920-30's.

If you think that Wallace Nutting furniture is expensive today, do two things:
1) Visit a reputable furniture store and inspect the prices of **brand new furniture**...furniture that doesn't even compare in quality or style with Wallace Nutting's.
2) Take one look at the **Shaker** or **Arts & Crafts** markets and ask yourself this question: Would I prefer to buy into those markets today...or should I have done it 10 years ago?

If you think Wallace Nutting furniture is expensive today, I can guarantee you one thing: **it won't get any cheaper.**

6) There is still enough Wallace Nutting Furniture around today to furnish an entire room, or an entire home. Wallace Nutting furniture is not easy to find today, but it is still available... if you look hard enough. If you were ever interested in furnishing an entire setting with the correct style and look, you can still do it today.

7) Wallace Nutting furniture is practically classified as "antique" in its own right today. Technically antiques are considered items that are at least 100 years old. With the earliest Nutting furniture being produced in 1917, some Nutting furniture is already over 70 years old. That means 70 years of wear...and 70 years of patina. You have the look and feel of old furniture...with the strength and durability of new.

8) And perhaps most importantly of all, this furniture has the added-value of its association with the most famous name in American antiques - WALLACE NUTTING. And that name is right there for everyone to see...Paper Label or Branded Signature.

Collectors collect the name. If there are two similar pieces of glass, one marked **Tiffany** and one unmarked, which will the collector want? Two similar pieces of porcelin, one marked **Meissen** and one unmarked? Two similar paintings, one marked **Van Gogh** and one unmarked?

The Wallace Nutting name is there for everyone to see..a name that is associated with Quality...Antiques...and Americana. No one in the history of American antiques has ever accomplished the types of things done by Wallace Nutting;

* he sold nearly 10,000,000 pictures, all bearing his name
* he published nearly 20 books, all bearing his name
* he gathered one of the most extensive collections of important antique furniture ever assembled... still on display in a major institution...still bearing his name
* he reproduced thousands of the finest pieces of furniture ever made, all bearing his name

I think Bill Bowers said it best in Chapter 10... *"One might say that Wallace Nutting contributed more for the preservation of our past heritage of American Arts and Culture than anyone else. We had greater names in the Arts, but they reached relatively few. Wallace Nutting was for everybody and everyone appreciated him. He put everything he had, both finances and all his time, to explain how and why our ancestors lived and felt. Our great musuems and names like Henry DuPont at Winterthur, are unquestionably the* *epitome of quality and taste...but these are the results of many millions of dollars and the employment of well-trained personnel. Our best institutions are the sum total of many people working at it full time and having umlimited amounts of money. **Wallace Nutting did it first...and single-handedly.**"*

Most experts agree that the finest examples of antique furniture are unobtainable to most collectors. The best examples are either in museums or private collections. When something great comes into the market, it usually is sold privately with few people even aware of the transaction. Or, the item is sold at Sotheby's, Christie's, or another well-known auction gallery for top dollar.

Today, more and more collectors are opting to avoid the repaired pieces with less than desirable form in favor of 20th century bench-made reproducions, made by a well known name.There are other 20th century furniture makers who also produced great furniture...Margolis...Kittenger...Fineberg...Stickley...but none produced the variety or overall quality of Wallace Nutting...and none have a name as universally recognizable as **Wallace Nutting.**

There is a word in the English language called **synergy.** Quite simply defined, this means than the total effect of an action is greater than the sum of its individual parts. This is what's happening to the Wallace Nutting market today.

* The Wallace Nutting picture market, by itself, has become a major market.
* There are nearly 20 different books written by Wallace Nutting being widely collected today.
* The Wadsworth Atheneum and Charter Oaks Temple Gallery, both in Hartford, Connecticut have had special Wallace Nutting Exhibitions. Other exhibitions by major institutions are sure to follow.

* Nutting Furniture is now being sold by such notable auction houses as Skinner's and Sotheby's.
* There are regular Wallace Nutting specialty auctions taking place which have become the center of Wallace Nutting activity.
* Collectors are even producing such unique items as Wallace Nutting Calendars, Wallace Nutting Christmas Cards, and Wallace Nutting Greeting Cards.

These separate and independant markets each have one thing in common...the name **Wallace Nutting**. Each of these markets, both high end and low end, are reinforcing each other, and calling attention to each other. This is a fascinating marketplace phenomenon and should be very interesting to observe in the coming years.

Wallace Nutting. It's the synergy of the name...it's the inter-relationship of the different markets...it's the diverse combination of high and low end collectors...that is causing the widespread attention to the Wallace Nutting market.

As always, the spotlight will eventaully shift to another area. It always has...it always will.

But, a strong Wallace Nutting market will remain. Because the name Wallace Nutting means **quality**...it means **style**...it means **Americana**.

Americana is here to stay. And so is Wallace Nutting.

WALLACE NUTTING

A New Catalogue of

REPRODUCTIONS

Just Issued

168 Pages; 500 objects shown
Very rich in new material

Price, $2.00
In three-quarter cloth, $3.00

WALLACE NUTTING
46 Park Street
FRAMINGHAM, MASSACHUSETTS

Advertisement for the 1930 Furniture Catalog

WALLACE NUTTING

Will talk on Old Furniture in the Lecture Room

at the

PHILADELPHIA ANTIQUES EXPOSITION

Illustrated by colored screen pictures in great number and variety

EVERY AFTERNOON AT HALF PAST TWO

Beginning Tuesday, May Third

And will exhibit many of his exquisite Colonial reproductions. The addresses, however, will make no reference to them.

Dummy and prospectus of the new work on furniture details and designs will also be shown and subscriptions taken. A thousand sketches.

These features were a notable element of interest at the New York Antiques Exposition.

Advertisement for a Wallace Nutting Furniture Lecture,
where he also publicized his reproductions

ABOUT THE AUTHOR

Michael Ivankovich has been collecting Wallace Nutting pictures, books, and furniture for more than 15 years. Like many collectors, he first began collecting Wallace Nutting's hand-colored pictures. The pictures led to Wallace Nutting books...and then to Wallace Nutting furniture. Today he is the largest collector/dealer of Wallace Nutting in the country.

This specialization in Wallace Nutting pictures led to his first book in 1984, **The Price Guide to Wallace Nutting Pictures**. A 2nd edition was released in 1986, a 3rd edition in 1989, and a 4th edition is scheduled for a 1991 release.

In 1987, he published **The Wallace Nutting Expansible Catalog**. This reprint of Wallace Nutting's 1915 Salesmen's Picture Catalog was an immediate hit and quickly became an invaluable tool to all serious Wallace Nutting collectors.

In 1988, he published **The Alphabetical and Numerical Index to Wallace Nutting Pictures**. This definitive 310 page book contains 10,000+ Wallace Nutting picture titles, along with various other essential information useful in authenticating and researching Wallace Nutting pictures.

A frequent lecturer on Wallace Nutting, Mr. Ivankovich has written articles for most major trade papers, has appeared on various radio and television programs, and is frequently consulted by antique columnists throughout the country. As part of his antique business he provides Wallace Nutting Appraisal Services, exhibits at various Antique Shows, and conducts regular Wallace Nutting Auctions throughout the Northeast.

The Guide to Wallace Nutting Furniture culminates more than 10 years of research into Wallace Nutting Furniture. Mr. Ivankovich is currently working on a book focusing upon other Wallace Nutting-like photographers from the early 1900's.

Michael Ivankovich is also the author of the book **The Strategy of Pitching Slow Pitch Softball**, and the writer/producer of a full length video by the same title...a diverse combination with Wallace Nutting to say the least. Together with his wife Susan, their company is a leader in the sale of Softball books and videos throughout the country.

They currently reside in Doylestown, PA with their four children, Nash, Jenna, Lindsey, and Megan. He can be reached at P.O. Box 2458, Doylestown, PA 18901, or by calling (215) 345-6094.

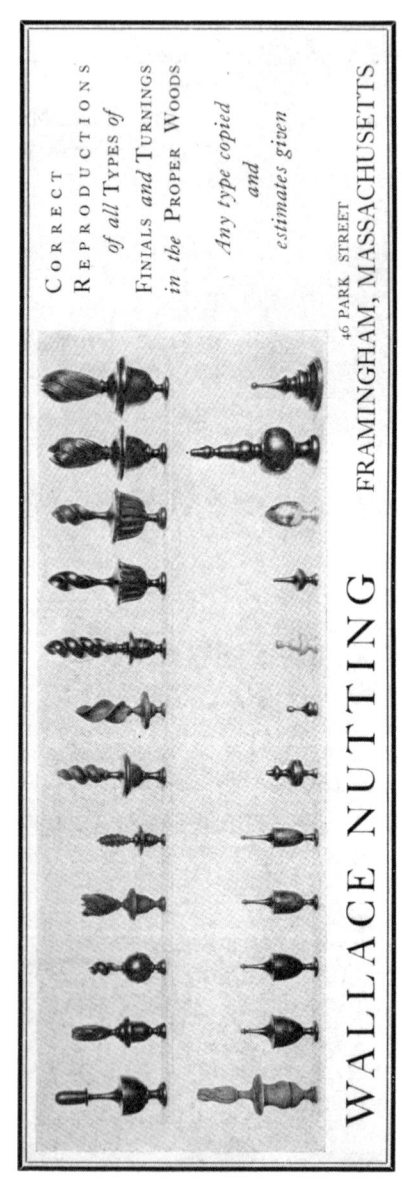

Wallace Nutting even reproduced items as small as finials